A MORE PERFECT
DEMOCRACY

A MORE PERFECT DEMOCRACY:

MODERNIZING THE UNITED STATES CONSTITUTION FOR THE 21ST CENTURY

RAYMOND LEO BLAIN, M.D., M.P.A.

*A More Perfect Democracy: Modernizing
the United States Constitution for the 21st Century*

For information about this title or to order other books
and/or electronic media, contact the publisher:

RLBlain Publishing, LLC
PO BOX 224
Roseville, CA 95661

ISBNs:
979-8-9887261-2-8 (hardcover)
979-8-9887261-0-4 (softcover)
979-8-9887261-1-1 (eBook)

Printed in the United States of America

Cover and Interior Design: 1106 Design

Table of Contents

Introduction

Most Americans have been brought up to respect the
Constitution as a superb document that, when written in 1787, estab-
lished a new form of government: A Federal Democratic Republic.
Time has proven that it did *not* establish a true democracy.

The Founding Fathers experimented first with a loose Confederation
of States, which quickly became apparent as too weak for the 18th
century, let alone modern times. So each of the original states sent
three delegates to Philadelphia to fix the Confederation. Fixing the
Confederation proved to be virtually impossible, so after much ran-
cor, they settled on the 1787 Constitution, with many loopholes and
vagaries, so that each side felt its interpretations were correct. New
Hampshire's approval resulted in the number of votes necessary for
ratification of the document in 1788. History has proven that such a
document could, and did, lead to many disputes and even a bloody and
vicious civil war. Remnants of that acrimonious dispute have percolated
below and periodically broken through to the surface ever since. Today
we are experiencing mass shooting events regularly, which I believe
are, in some cases, a guerrilla attempt at a continuation of our civil war.

It certainly must seem presumptuous that a physician with only limited training and experience in law or politics would attempt such a monumental task as rewriting a document that is the foundation and source of our political and legal structure. Perhaps a brief summary about me and my beliefs would help.

I was born into a family of two parents, five brothers, counting me, and two sisters, toward the end of the Great Depression, in the industrial city of Holyoke, Massachusetts. The Great Depression began the industrial, economic, and social decline of that city's very prosperous days, like that of many American cities of commerce. We lived in Lyman Terrace, one of two public-housing projects, until I was fourteen years old, saving us from the humiliation and hardship of living in one of the many Hoovervilles, where the homeless struggled to survive. My father had dropped out of school in 7th grade. We older siblings started our working careers as teenagers in a delicatessen. I worked illegally at age fourteen. My starting pay was $0.60/hour, so a 40-hour week paid $24 minus state, federal, and social-security taxes. Take-home pay was about $18, most of which went to assisting with family expenses and saving for future education.

With federal assistance, working, and borrowed money, I was one of three who attended college and two who finished graduate school. We were probably a typical family of our generation. I offer this example to emphasize how much life has changed even just in my lifetime, yet we still live in a country with a constitution that was written for how life was almost 250 years ago.

I served in the U.S. Air Force from April 1966 to June 30, 1972, while war raged in Southeast Asia. I practiced medicine for seventeen years in a private pediatric practice and for fifteen years as a full-time medical-policy consultant for the State of California, during which time I received my Master's Degree in Public Administration. Mine is a very common American generational history. I mention these so that our younger generation can compare their experiences to those of ours. My experiences were neither exceptional nor rare. We were brought up to love this country and work to make it a more fraternal, equal, and democratic place to prosper and raise future citizens both native and naturalized.

During my four-score-plus years, I have had an interest in history, politics, the Constitution, the social, legal, and technological transformation of our country, and its politics, health, culture, and economy. The transformations have been remarkable, and the pace for change has quickened, making the 1787 Constitution more obsolete and prone to more rapid and widespread abuse. Changes on the horizon promise even-more-challenging political, social, ethnic, ethical, security, and survival issues.

I am an average American who has worked hard for his country and fellow citizens. I have never held political office. I am not wealthy. I am not a lawyer. You and I love our country. We both want peace, stability, justice, equality, freedom, and safety to prevail. Who better to try to create a modern Constitution with these as the primary goals than one of us? Who has less, and, in some ways, more, to gain with the creation of a better Constitution and truer democracy?

Of course, you will agree with some of the many changes I have included and probably disagree with others, but I ask you to give each part careful consideration, not solely for your own wishes but what would be best for the United States as a whole and the greatest majority of its citizens. It is part of the intrinsic makeup of a true democracy that (to paraphrase a remark attributed to Abraham Lincoln and quoted to me by others) "You can please some of the people most of the time, most of the people some of the time, but you can never please all of the people all of the time." I would add that it may even be possible to please *none* of the people sometimes. I believe these are the people who would prefer an aristocracy, with a privileged minority ruling class, or a monarchy or dictatorship. People who favor aristocracy or dictatorship will never fit comfortably in a democracy but must be required to accept its decisions or exercise their freedom to move elsewhere. If a significant part of this new document is to your liking, I would ask that you invite your family and friends to also read the book, and petition Congress to consider adopting this document before or after making any objective and fair changes that would improve it.

As a physician, I see the United States today as a patient that has been exploited, bled for selfish power and wealth, mishandled, suffering from a broken and damaged skeleton, with a weakened heart, deliberate memory loss about the good and bad in our history because of denial and self-deceit, suffering from a rising temperature due to self-inflicted perceived grievance, hatred, racism, fascism, autocracy, a white-supremacy myth, and self-righteousness. Our beloved country is headed to the Intensive Care Unit unless it is helped by massive infusions of modern thinking by its citizens, adaptations to handle the modern world, and excision of ideas, systems, or structures that are now doing more harm than good to our goal of having a true democracy. A new Constitution is necessary. A few more Band-Aid amendments will not save the patient.

The final chapter of this book is a copy of the 1787 Constitution and its amendments to date as published on the Internet with its original spelling and lettering by the National Constitution Center, 525 Arch St., Philadelphia, Pennsylvania. It is included so that the reader can judge independently the validity of the remarks I will be making about it and why a new, more-modern Constitution is critically needed as soon as possible to save our snail's pace movement toward true democracy. Recent decades have been plagued by a drift to severe partisan politics, authoritarianism, and destruction of what we used to think were checks and balances among the three Branches of the United States Federal Government. These are movements *away from* democracy.

Most chapters are discussions of what the 1787 Constitution actually says and establishes my thinking behind why the new text is suggested in the offered document. My justifications for the changes are in the areas of discussion, and some of the pros and cons that I believe might arise in *a discussion of my reasons for these revisions. What I have added or revised will be in bold italic.*

Another begins with a discussion of a different way of looking at the structure of Congress and subsurface forces that may have been behind why it was created the way it was. There is a discussion of how the new text I am suggesting would decrease the ambiguity of parts of Article I of the 1787 Constitution, the structure, inequities, powers, and limitations we have been living under, the abuses that have infiltrated it like a cancer—abuses at the federal and state levels of its provisions—and suggestions for remediation and the justifications thereof, that have come to my mind after decades of observation, greater understanding, and concern.

After considering the Preamble, we deal with Article I, II and III with their issues and corruptions that have altered power and weakened the balance of powers we were led to accept that the Legislative, Executive, and Judicial Branches were supposed to have. We thought these checks and balances would prevent abuses by the occupants of each Branch and their subordinates. They have not.

The discussions and changes go on to deal similarly with Article III and the Judiciary, and its control and corruption by outside forces.

The twentieth chapter is the New Constitution for the 21st Century as a unified document that I offer for the American political system—but especially for its citizens—to consider, debate, change and, adopt—or reject by Congress and the States, or in a national plebiscite, as a last resort. We are divided by those wanting a true democracy and those favoring complete control of power with an aristocracy and dictator, something our outgoing President George Washington warned us to fear more than 200 years ago. Choose—or pay the consequences.

★　★　★

CHAPTER 1

A Brief Background History to the American Revolution and the Current 1787 Constitution

In order to get sufficient votes of the delegates to the 1787 (Confederation of States) Convention and get nine of the original States to ratify the 1787 Constitution that emerged, the document contained the result of many compromising provisions that were not explicitly defined, so that the delegates could develop their own individual interpretations and justify their vote or approval. Several States also demanded the addition of the First Ten Amendments (the Bill of Rights) before voting to accept the document.

But knowing this is not enough to see, below the surface, other factors that probably played a significant role in how it was written.

The Role of an Emerging Aristocracy.

Since the early days of the voyages of Columbus, slavery became an integral part of the early economies of North and South America, especially in areas with predominantly agrarian economies. Many owners developed large slave-labor plantations; merchant businesses in England were often importers and sellers of our production to European consumers. In turn, the newly emerging entrepreneurs in the colonies wanted to live like and be aristocrats. Many bought European products so that their lifestyle could, over time, mimic those of European aristocrats and minor royalty.

Unfortunately for many, their purchases spent more than their sales covered, and, thus, they became indebted. For the thirteen colonies, this happened especially in the more agrarian southern areas, but no area was immune. Pennsylvania and states to the north were beginning to emerge slowly from cottage industries which would eventually challenge English manufacturing.

Simultaneously, the French in Canada began to move to and claim lands in the Ohio Valley. The English became aware that a French military force was traveling to build a fort in what is now Pittsburgh. The more this progressed, the more France would have a strong claim to the Ohio valley. Many of the budding colonial aristocracy had also begun claiming land in the Ohio valley, hoping to be able to sell that land to settlers moving westward and thus generate extra income to pay off their English debts. In England, the king and Parliament did not want the French moving into areas between the Mississippi and Appalachia, and adding those areas to their massive holdings in what would eventually become known as the Louisiana Purchase.

The Virginia House of Burgesses decided to honor the king's wishes to block the French and authorized George Washington to lead a militia force to meet the French force and negotiate their withdrawal without building a fort. Along the way, Native-American warriors joined Washington's small force. When this combined force came upon a smaller group of French soldiers, instead of negotiation, hostilities ensued (who fired the first shot is a subject for historical debate). The French unit was forced to retreat, with some atrocities committed against them (some believe) by the Native-American warriors in Washington's force. The force attacked by the Americans turned out to only be a patrol, and, when the main French force came after Washington's militia, they wisely retreated back to Virginia. Thus began the French and Indian War, with a large part of the military and financial burden of that war falling on the English.

England eventually won, acquiring Canada. The Proclamation of 1763 by the English king denied crossing the Appalachian mountains for settlement to the people of the thirteen colonies.[1] Native Americans probably assumed that no Europeans would cross the Appalachian Mountains and be allowed to settle permanently there, including the Ohio Valley, so the hopes of the indebted colonial aristocracy's plan to get out of debt was destroyed.

The English also decided that the colonists should help pay part of the cost of the war, so they applied taxes on the importing of English products by the colonies, like the tea tax, without meaningful representation in Parliament for the colonists.

These additional facts may influence your understanding of the causes and results of the American Revolution as being more complex than we were originally taught. I remember reading that historians believed that the maximum number of colonists who favored the Revolution never exceeded 45%, with many switching sides several times during the eight years of the Revolution, depending upon who was perceived as winning at a particular time. The remainder of the colonists were neutral or favored not revolting.[2]

The mixed loyalties, education, wealth, and the political and social aspirations of the newly independent colonists probably had important, if not conscious, influence on the eventual provisions of the 1787 Constitution. I inferred from my readings that the emerging upper caste did not fully trust the loyalty or judgment of many of their fellow poor and uneducated fellow citizens. So, they built into our constitutions provisions that gave an imagined superior aristocracy supervisory and even veto power over the majority, as exemplified by the original selection of Senators by State politicians, impeachment trial by political Senators, and the rapid creation of the Electoral College for selecting—and possible overriding of the popular vote—the President and Vice President, in the Twelfth Amendment, the second following the Bill of Rights.

The 1787 Constitution also created a special larger jury of politicians two times the number of states, currently 100 jurors) for Impeachments than the juries for ordinary citizens (12 for murder).

I have chosen to include, as the last chapter, the text of the 1787 Constitution and all the Amendments so that you can read it for yourself and decide if it really created a true democracy—one that is still appropriate and effective for meeting the desires of the citizens of the United States in modern times, especially in light of all of the significant changes that have brought us to the 21st century.

★ ★ ★

The 1787 Constitution, the Emerging Aristocracy, and the Structure of Congress

BEFORE DISCUSSING THE CHANGES being suggested for **Article I, Section 1** as written in the 1787 Constitution, it would be profitable to step back and look at what the structure says about what the Founding Fathers' motives may have been that determined the course they took.

The Revolutionary Army did poorly most of the eight-year duration of that struggle. If the revolt had failed, there would likely have been a large number of executions, imprisonments, confiscation of property, and other degrees of punishment for anyone who had fought or supported the insurrection. The war ended because we had worn down the British resolve and treasury, and acquired powerful allies in France and Spain. The newly independent colonies formed a confederation. It failed for many reasons but especially because the States did not want to surrender their independence to a central government.

In England, the king was the chief executive, but Parliament shared power. Parliament consisted of two Houses: The House of

Lords were people with an hereditary title, money, education, and some political influence; The House of Commons was for the less-educated or uneducated, emerging middle class. Parliament still echoes that past, but so does our Congress. Look again at Article I of our existing Constitution as it was originally written.

The House of Representatives is similar to the House of Commons. Its members were more likely to be less educated and less wealthy; they were chosen to represent groups composed overwhelmingly of laborers, shopkeepers, and non-college graduates. This has been slowly changing as more citizens get more education and as the middle class has grown.

The original Senate was not chosen directly by the people. Each State received two members, regardless of population. The justification usually used is that this was to balance the power, so that the States with large populations would not dominate any decision-making. If the Founding Fathers had wanted a true democracy, where everyone's vote is equal, this would not have been done. For example, California has almost 39,000,000 people, but each of the Dakotas, and Wyoming, have fewer than 1,000,000. California gets a more proportional membership in the House of Representatives than in the Senate, where all three of these less-populous States still get two Senators each—just like California. So, a California Senator represents about thirty-nine people for every one represented in the other three States. To be truly Democratic (one person = one vote, with all votes having equal power for the people), the Senate should be set up just like the House of Representatives—with each State's number of Senators based on population.

To amplify this maldistribution of power and to provide political control of the Senate, in 1787, Senators were picked by State Legislatures—not the vote of the people—until the Seventeenth Amendment.

To further prevent the People from having a true democracy, the 12th Amendment established the Electoral College (which *still* actually selects our chief executives), which is rightly seen as a restriction that denies the People the right to directly elect the President and Vice President. You and I have only an *indirect* vote, because, when we vote, we are only picking the Electors from our State, who then do the actual voting for the President. If you don't believe me, read the current 12th Amendment for yourself. To make matters worse, the rules governing how electors vote varies by State and political party. Some States have "winner-take-all" rules; so, if in State #1, which has three electoral votes and the winning candidate gets 254,678 popular votes to the losing candidate's 254,677, the winning candidate would get *all three Electoral votes.* Conversely, if State #2 does *not* have "winner-take-all" rules but, instead, has proportional-voting rules, and the winning candidate garners a margin of only one popular vote, the winning candidate would get only two of the three Electoral votes, and the losing candidate would still get one.

In some states, the Electors can ignore the popular vote *completely.* In those States, the Electors could give all the Electoral votes to one party if they wanted to, *even if the other party's candidate got the majority of popular votes.* Currently State legislatures make the rules for federal elections, so the rules are not the same everywhere. The picture is getting even darker in some States, because the state legislatures in those States are considering passing laws to give themselves the power to overturn *any results they don't like.*

It is time for the Constitution to give voters the same representation ratios in both the House *and* the Senate, as would be the case in a *true* "representative democracy" and to at least reserve the power of making rules for *federal* elections solely for *federal* lawmakers.

I have been told that, when Benjamin Franklin was asked after the Constitutional Convention of 1787 what kind of government we would be having, he answered "A federal republic, if we can keep it." If that is true, then he never said we would be a democracy, but we have lived for almost two hundred and fifty years thinking we were. In these perilous times, when we may lose what we have to an aristocracy of a rich, powerful, and biased minority, isn't it time to write a new Constitution that makes us a democracy and eliminates loopholes that allow some to exploit our government for their own selfish goals of increasing wealth and power?

What follows are my suggestions for restoring much of the balance of power between and within the three Branches of our Federal government, making our Federal government more democratic, more ethical, more equally representative, more responsive to the will of citizens like you and me, giving the people the final say in what our laws and courts do, giving you and me the right to recall politicians who defy the will of the people in favor of their own desires and power, and the voting power to overturn Supreme Court decisions that are contrary to the will of the People. If you agree with these goals, please read what follows with an open mind and the goal of what is best for the country as a whole and not just our individual desires.

★ ★ ★

CHAPTER 3

Revisions and Additions
to a More Perfect Democracy:
Modernizing the United States Constitution
for the 21st Century

Preamble

We, the People of the United States of America, *now live in a different world than when our original Constitution was written in 1787 and adopted in 1788. Many unforeseen events, customs, ethical variations, political institutions, social, economic, technological, and population changes have transpired in the interim. Therefore, it is necessary to bring the Constitution of the United States into the 21st century with modernizing revisions to better define and protect the rights and responsibilities of all citizens,* in order to form an *even* more perfect *Democracy*, provide for the common domestic and foreign defense, *promote the general Health, Welfare, Rights, and Safety, and to secure the maximum* Blessings of Liberty. *In the interests of Equality and Justice to ourselves and future posterity, we ordain and adopt this more modern Constitution of the United States of America.*

Discussion of Justification

Pros:

It has become apparent that, in order to continue to form a more perfect union and democracy, prevent repetition of abuses and misinterpretations of the original document, and correct imbalances that have occurred among the three Branches since 1788, the Constitution needs clearer and more precise language in 21st-century American English to delineate the purposes of the Constitution and the structure, selection, duties, responsibilities, and limitations of the three Branches of the federal government.

1. 200+ years of changes in the diversity of our population, customs, laws, and interpretations of laws and reasoning behind them necessitate more delineation and clarity;

2. Public consensus has emerged, although not unanimous, that healthcare, basic housing, freedom from hunger, formal or occupational education, easy access and opportunity for voting, equality, and safety from verbal, physical, technological, or lethal-weapon assault in all public and private places controlled by United States federal, state, territorial, or military jurisdictions are, or must be, guaranteed rights, and we need safeguards to the democratic ideals to which most Americans aspire at all levels of government in the United States of America;

3. It has been known to the public in general, that the United States has incarcerated individuals thought to be serious security risks in facilities in foreign countries without benefit of a court hearing or trial. This is against international law and the 1787 Constitution, and must be clearly forbidden in the future. Charge them, give them trials, or send them back to

where they came from. If we violate the Constitution against them, what is to prevent its violation against any of us? I hate terrorists, but everyone should be given a fair and timely trial.

4. Any person detained in any facility under the jurisdiction of the United States must be charged with a crime within the lawful time required, provided competent legal representation, or released, because:
    i. That person is suspected of being guilty, and there is believed to be sufficient evidence for a speedy trial by a judge and jury;
    ii. That person may be guilty, but there is insufficient evidence to prove it, in which case, we do not have legal or moral justification for continued confinement; if not a citizen, that person must be immediately deported back to their point of departure to the United States,
    iii. That person is innocent, and incarceration is unlawful.

5. For decades, foreigners have been coming to the United States with serious illnesses, and, under American law, claiming care at American expense upon arrival;

6. People visiting the United States or seeking asylum or immigrant status should be protected with the same humane dignity and human rights while here, except voting rights, which are reserved for citizens, in keeping with International and American Human Rights Law and tradition.

7. All visitors, visa holders, and immigrants should be required to enroll and pay *pro rata* fees for the same care and services covered for citizens while in the United States or any of its possessions or territories for the duration of the period each

is present if more than 24 hours, even if in transit. American taxpayers should not be abused by foreigners or travelers who come here seeking free care for illnesses, injuries, hereditary or congenital conditions, or conditions that happen or are discovered after they arrive, at the sole expense of Americans. Congress needs the unconditional authority to and should enact such legislation. If our representatives in Congress, Chief Executives, and judges do not do their duty, the people should have recourse to recall them.

★ ★ ★

CHAPTER 4

Revisions to Article I:
The Legislative Branch: The House of Representatives

ARTICLE I

Section 1: The Legislative Branch

All legislative Powers herein granted shall be vested in a Congress of the United States, which shall consist of a Senate and House of Representatives. *No laws shall be made by the Executive or Judicial Branches by decree or judicial decision, except when granted by a law of Congress which specifies the duration and limits of the temporary authority established by both Houses of Congress. These Executive Orders or Temporary Court Decisions allowed may be made permanent by Congress as a new law before the temporary-authority period ends, otherwise, all laws and executive orders issued under this temporary authority become inactive and unenforceable after the Sunset Date set when the temporary authority was established. The Judicial Branch shall not decide the intent of a law since it did not make the Law. Only Congress can specify the intent, and if this is not clear, the Judicial Branch should send the law back to the Legislative Branch for clarification of the intent within the law.*

Discussion of Justification for Changes

Pros:

Since the 1787 Constitution was adopted, there have been many examples of the Judiciary making Law by case precedent or by ruling that only parts of a Law are unconstitutional, even though the Constitution never granted or permitted such power in writing to the Judicial Branch. The original wording of the Constitution limits the power to make laws solely to Congress. This 21st-century Constitution emphasizes that those powers are not shared with the other two Branches, except when Congress shall so authorize and only with specified limitations as to subject and duration of the authorization, as, for instance, when a temporary emergency occurs such as an insurrection or disaster. An example would be in a President imposing Martial Law. This provision restores more balance between the Executive and Legislative Branches and Judiciary than currently exists.

If a federal court decides a specific civil or criminal case on the facts of that case, it should not apply to any other similar cases unless Congress makes it a Law. English Common law may have allowed this, but our current Constitution mentions common law (in the 7th Amendment) only for cases of minor-value situations. All similar cases must be decided by an individual, independent judge or jury based on the facts of the new case until a specific Law is passed, if none exists. This prevents the Judicial Branch from making Law by case precedent. This restores more Balance of Power between the Legislative and Judicial Branches, as was originally intended.

This new provision in the 21st-century Constitution insists on maintenance of the separation of powers, except for limited times and limited areas of Law, and only when specifically authorized by Congress for temporary emergencies.

This position puts additional pressure on Congress to do its job and make Laws when needed.

When such cases are appealed to higher courts under this more specific Constitution, which limits the lawmaking ability of the Judicial Branch, judges and juries will have to make the decision on the facts of that individual case, and their decision will not become case law (a *de facto* new law) even at the Supreme Court level. A Constitutional amendment or new law will be necessary to change this provision for all similar cases or issues.

If Congress does not make such a Law, then:

a. Congress has decided that such a Law is not needed;
b. Congress is not doing its job, and Members of Congress need to be replaced by vote of the people for new Members who will do their job;
c. A constitutional amendment can change this limitation.

Section 2: The House of Representatives

Subsection 2a) Term of Office

The House of Representatives shall be composed of Members chosen every *four years* by a majority of citizens with the right to vote in a *Congressional Representation District. The Congressional Representation Districts shall be established by the National Federal Redistricting Board, established by Section 3 of this Article and delineated as equally as possible, based on population data from the most recent national census, within each of the several States for each election.*

The names and total votes for every candidate for federal office from all Federal Congressional Representation Districts shall be sent to the Executive of the State, in which case they are to be certified and forwarded to the National Redistricting Board headquarters in the federal capital for counting in the presence of at least one Representative of the House, Senate, Executive, and Judiciary Branches and determining the winners of seats in each district. The Board will then notify the candidates, the President, the Speaker of the House, and the President of the Senate, and appropriate media, of the results.

Subsection 2b) Procedure for Beginning New Four-Year Terms
Immediately after they shall be assembled in consequence of the first election, all Members elected to the House of Representatives shall be divided into two classes by the Federal National Redistricting Board, with the number of members of a political party in each class as equal as possible. The Representatives of the first Class who were reelected shall begin their term of office, as usual, at the end of the recent two-year term and serve for two more years. New members in this class will serve only two years before their seat is again up for election. Those of the second Class shall begin on the same date but continue for the new term length of four years.

Thereafter, all terms shall have a length of four years unless terminated by impeachment, recall by the voters, resignation, illness, or death, or other malfeasance, dereliction of duties, violation of oath of office, or conviction for a felony that would impede the ability of the Member to perform the duties of their office. If vacancies happen before the next scheduled election for that position, and more than 120 days remain in that term, the Executive of the State shall appoint a Temporary Interim Representative from the same political party as the vacated Member to fill the position until the next regularly scheduled election for the House for that position.

Discussion of Justification for the Changes

Pros:

Currently, Members of the House of Representative are all chosen every two years; this has several disadvantages:

a. Voters can change the character of the House of Representatives only once every 24 months, since there is no recall provision.

b. With House elections occurring every two years for all House Members, it has become necessary for those who currently wish to have more than one term to start fundraising immediately on taking office and begin campaigning for reelection shortly thereafter. This requires valuable time that would be better spent in committee hearings, chamber sessions debating and voting, and in researching and writing legislation. This new proposal—of four-year terms for the House of Representatives—will result in Members having more time to do the job of Representative since they will have to run for office only once every four years unless their seat is eliminated after a one-in-ten-year census or they are recalled by the people they are supposed to be representing.

A similar reapportionment process happens now, as populations shift and the number of House districts in a State has to be adjusted. With four-year terms, there may be more Members who have their term shortened if a State loses seats, but that number should not be large and may be less disruptive than it is now.

The equal representation of each Representative would still not be perfect, but it would be as fair as possible while still giving small-population States at least one Representative, as is currently done.

Cons:
The first Class-one seats may remain in office for only two years' duration for the first term after the new duration of House terms begins, so that the staggered four-year terms can begin.

Subsection 2c) Size House of Representatives

The total number of Members of the House of Representatives shall not exceed 450. Each Representative shall represent an approximately equal number of people as closely as possible while not exceeding the total limit of 450 Members in the House of Representatives.

Discussion of Justification for the Changes

Pros:
The number of citizens represented of each Representative would still not be perfect but as fair as possible while still giving small-population States at least one Representative as is currently done. Allowing 450 Members is to allow both the House and Senate to accommodate the admission of new States.

If the total number of members of either the House or the Senate grows without limit, the chambers could become so large that the number of new bills to be considered, the amount of time to consider Amendments, the amount of time allowed for debate so that every Member can express the views and desires of their constituents, and the time to vote on each measure would become ineffective and unwieldy. 450 Members is not much larger than the current limit.

Subsection 2d) Qualifications for Representatives

No Person shall be a Representative who shall not have attain*ed the age* of *eighteen years and been six years a citizen of the United States.*

A person may seek elective office to the House of Representatives only if that person has resided in a congressional district in which that person has legally maintained primary residence for a minimum of 365 days before the election and continues to maintain primary residence for the entire term of representation. "Primary residence" shall mean physical occupation for 365 days each calendar year, except that days serving in the national capital shall also count as being in the primary residence. If a Member moves out of the district represented, that Member must immediately resign.

Discussion of Justification for Changes

Pros:
The current Twenty-Sixth Amendment guarantees the right to vote to all citizens eighteen and older. If that person is considered mature and informed enough to pick from among the candidates, why shouldn't that person be allowed to be a candidate? The restriction is a holdover from the original aristocratic biases of some of the Founding Fathers and is no longer justifiable.

Recent history shows a growing tendency for people to run for office in a district or even States by moving to another location in the new district less than one year before the election. This is unfair to the valid residents of the Representation District in question. It seems justified to limit candidates to running only in a district where they have lived long enough to become familiar with the issues of importance to the people in the voting district, because the candidate is supposed to represent the views in that district. One year of continued primary residency before, and continued, uninterrupted residence in that district for the entire term of office should be minimum standards for candidacy.

Subsection 2e) Filling Vacancies in the House of Representatives
When vacancies open in the Federal Congressional Representative District from any State, the Executive of that State shall order an election in the Federal District represented by the vacancy, to be held within 60 calendar days of the beginning of the vacancy unless fewer than 120 calendar days remain in the term of the vacancy. All candidates seeking to be elected to fill out the remainder of the vacant term must meet age and citizenship requirements, be free of any impediments established by federal law, and register with the State office in charge of elections at least 30 days before the election.

Discussion of Justification for the Changes

Pros:

With the new term duration of four years and the continuing Senate term duration of six years, unexpected early vacancies will occur from time to time because of death, illness, resignation, recall, or removal, so this provision allows emergency elections to refill the vacancy for the remainder of a term with more than 120 days remaining.

The Executive of the State should not appoint a replacement of a different political party from the person being replaced because the Executive may have political motives contrary to the wishes of the electorate, especially in cases of a successful recall.

Currently, unfinished terms in the House of Representatives can be filled by the Executive of the State by issuing a Writ for a new election to fill the vacant position, but there are no specified limits for when this must be done. If the empty seat was occupied by a member of a political party opposed to the current State Executive's political philosophy, the Executive could delay issuing the Writ until the next regularly scheduled federal election for that term, thus denying representation to the citizens for up to four years for the House and six years for the Senate. The modernized U.S. Constitution must establish time limits for the Writ, the filing for candidacy, campaigning, and for the date of final voting, since deadlines for these actions may not be specified in the State Constitution.

Subsection 2f) Choosing Speaker of the House of Representatives and Rules for Each Session of Congress

The House of Representatives shall choose their Speaker upon opening of each new Congress after all new members have been sworn in by the outgoing Speaker or new majority leader in the absence of the outgoing Speaker.

The Congress shall assemble at least every calendar year for a total of not less than 200 calendar days, except on Saturdays and Sundays unless they choose to meet more often. The House of Representatives and Senate may choose to allow virtual attendance and voting at committee and general sessions with necessary security provisions. The presence of a quorum of the House Membership shall be required to conduct any business, debate, or to give speeches. Closed-door sessions shall be limited to items of national security and in-person attendance only.

Discussion of Justification for the Changes

Pros:

This Constitution specifies that Members-elect must be sworn in before voting for Speaker of the House so that their vote for Speaker is always legal.

In recent years, Congress has had to wait for Members to arrive from their home districts in order to hold sessions, debate, and take votes. Modern technology should allow enough security for virtual attendance and voting except in special circumstances. This option should be left open for Congress to use.

Having debates and giving speeches when few are in attendance is a waste of time and taxpayer money. Members of Congress should have to be present except when there are conflicts such as committee meetings, hearings, or other special circumstances.

National-security issues should not be open, since open sessions can give information that could be useful to enemies.

★　★　★

CHAPTER 5

Revisions to Article I: Federal Congressional Redistricting Board

ARTICLE I

Section 3: Qualifications, Duties, and Procedure for Appointing Federal Congressional Redistricting Board Members and their Compensation

Subsection 3a) Qualification, Procedural, Terms of Office of Federal Congressional Redistricting Board Members

Determination of District boundaries for Federal Congressional Representatives shall be determined by a Federal Congressional Redistricting Board, consisting of two resident citizens of each State, nominated by the President and approved by a simple majority vote in both Houses of Congress, none of whom shall have held public office, been an officer of any political party, been convicted of any felony, been a political lobbyist, or engaged in any illegal activity with regard to any form of public service. Redistricting shall be completed within six months of completion of each official ten-year National Census and whenever circumstances so require. The first group shall be appointed in the first twelve months following adoption of this Constitution and serve a minimum term of ten years or longer but ending on the first day of January of the next year ending in "5" after at least 10 years of service. Each Board member appointed thereafter shall serve for ten years starting on the 1st of January in years ending in "5."

The goal of the Federal Congressional Redistricting Board within each State shall be to have the total of such districts within a State reflect the political, ethnic, and cultural composition of that State as closely as possible so that Members-elect sent to the House of Representatives and Senate will as closely as possible be based on the most recent census data. All voters in a Federal Congressional District must be in the same contiguous geographic area.

Discussion of Justification for Changes

Pros:

With this new Constitution, all States would have the same number of Members in the House of Representatives and the Senate, based on population (see discussion under Section 5), so that all people would have as close to a ONE PERSON—ONE VOTE POWER equality, because representation would be based on population in a democracy rather than just the status of being a State.

Redistricting should be done by people who are less likely to attempt gerrymandering, with the purpose of a more democratic election. For federal elections, the Federal Constitution should define the people responsible and the methods and purposes so that the criteria are as uniform as possible for all districts. Since Congress makes the federal laws for all the States and citizens, it is less likely to be as biased as those determined by political parties or a committee solely of citizens of the same State where the current and changeable preferences could be biased and can dominate the process of creating voting districts. The current process has demonstrated that, given the opportunity, there are politicians who would structure districts so as to usually allow dominance by one of the political parties. A committee to define voting boundaries that could affect Laws for all States and Citizens should have representatives from all states who represent all the types of constituents in that State. The two major political-party membership should be equal and independent, or third-party voters should be given tie-breaking votes when they serve as members.

Recent decades have demonstrated a trend of gerrymandering in an increasing number of States, making it more difficult for members of other political parties to win election. This is a clear violation of the one person-one vote foundation of a democracy. Since Congress makes laws that affect relationships between States and all the several States, it is reasonable to take the voting rules for federal offices and move them to the Congress.

By having two members from each state, any individual or group trying to bring bias into the proceedings will likely be discovered, exposed, and opposed in their efforts by a majority from other States, and the resulting redistricting should be as fair as possible within the rules.

Since national censuses occur in years ending in "0," having new members appointed in years ending in "5" will allow time to be able to learn the rules and procedures before the biggest workload occurs in the first years following a census.

This Section is to try to establish as unbiased and fair redistricting procedures as possible.

Subsection 3b)
Congress shall determine the annual compensation and travel and lodging allotments for Members to attend Federal Congressional Redistricting

Board meetings in the national capital. The members shall not accept any other form of compensation or emolument for activities related to their duties as Board members, or that might give the appearance of attempting to influence any member's decisions.

Subsection 3c)
The Congress shall have the Power to enforce this Section by appropriate legislation or by Constitutional Amendment.

Discussion of Justification for Changes

These two provisions are designed to try to minimize bribery and misuse of taxpayer funds and take into account increased costs due to inflation during a ten-year term.

★ ★ ★

CHAPTER 6

Article I
Section 4: Voter Recall of Members
of the House of Representatives or Senate

Section 4: Procedure for Voters to Recall a Member
of the House of Representatives, or Senate.

If 10 percent of the registered voters of a Congressional District sign a Petition for Recall for their elected Congressional Member and present this petition to the Office of the Governor of that State or equivalent territorial executive, that official shall call for a Special Recall Referendum and Replacement Vote to be held throughout that District or Territorial region represented by the Member within 60 calendar days of the date the Petition was presented if more than 120 calendar days remain in the term of that Member. Congressional candidates may participate as possible replacements as Representatives or Senators from that District by filing applications. All candidates seeking to be elected to fill out the remainder of the vacant term must meet age and citizenship requirements, be free of any impediments established by federal law, and register with the government office in charge of elections at least 30 days before the recall/

replacement election. Voters would then vote on a ballot containing a Yes/No vote on the Recall and a first and second choice for a replacement. If the final vote is a majority of Yes Votes for Recall, the new candidate with the most combined first- and second-choice votes will be elected to fill the remainder of the vacated position in the House of Representatives or Senate. If fewer than 120 days remain in the term, the seat shall remain vacant until the next regularly scheduled election for that seat in the House of Representatives.

Discussion of Justification for Changes

Pros:

1. Recent events have shown that Congressional Members are being retained so as to have a political party retain power who might otherwise be in jeopardy of removal, or even when the Member is indicted for multiple crimes. The argument being used is that the accused has not been found guilty. This is true, but the Member has publicly admitted telling falsehoods about his experience and credentials while running for office and has not been removed. Under the current system, the voters of that District have no recourse for removal now or even after a trial, which may not occur before that person's term is finished. The people the Representative is supposed to speak for currently have no direct recourse to remove that Member if they wish to do so at any time during that person's term, for any cause. This needs to be changed. Many States have recall-petition provisions for State officials; it is time to have such provisions for federal recall now that we are in the 21st century.

2. The process must not be too easy or too difficult so that it is abused or never attempted. The 1787 Constitution offers no such option, and candidates have engaged in the abuses mentioned, with the voters helpless to remove them. With the longer terms of this new Constitution, it is even more important to implement the possibility of removal by the voters—and not just by Impeachment.

3. Some States already have Recall provisions in their Constitutions for State office holders, even the Executive. Congress and Supreme Court judges should likewise be subject to recall when they violate the will of a majority of the voters, so this new Constitution includes this provision if we are to be a true democracy.

★　★　★

CHAPTER 7

Section 5:
Federal Impeachment

Power of Impeachment of any federal office holder in Congress, the Executive, or Judicial Branch, regardless of how that person was elected, appointed, or otherwise came to occupy their position of public service, shall be possible by the House of Representatives or Senate.

Subsection 5b) Impeachment Trials

Judgement in Cases of Impeachment of any federal official elected or hired shall, henceforth, be by a jury of twelve citizens selected in the manner of all other criminal proceedings, since all citizens must be treated as Equals before the Law, and not be influenced by political bias. If found guilty, punishment shall be according to Law for the offense, except in cases of treason or espionage, when the punishment shall be life in prison without pardon or parole. Treason shall constitute giving aid or comfort to an enemy of the United States of America that threatens the national security in time of peace or war, except as part of federal-government-sanctioned negotiations for a treaty of peace, or end of hostilities.

Discussion of Justification for the Changes

Pros:

1. In the past, initiation of impeachment proceedings has been limited to the House of Representatives because the House acted as a Grand Jury in such proceedings, and the Senate acted as the trial Jury. This more modern Constitution, in seeking to approach greater equality before the law, moves the impeachment trial to a jury of peer citizens rather than politicians.

2. The Senate thus can become co-equal with the House of Representatives in initiating impeachment proceedings and in having a temporary committee to investigate, similar to a Grand Jury. Recent events have also demonstrated that either house of the Congress may be reluctant to investigate or punish transgressions by one of its own members.

3. This new provision allows the House or Senate to initiate impeachment proceedings of any government official, including the Senate, against a Member of the House when the House fails to do so, thus removing from the House a singular ability to protect its own from investigation and/or punishment.

Subsection 5c) Grounds for Impeachment
Charges for Impeachment shall include but not be limited to:

1. *Repeated false or misleading campaign statements;*

2. *Misuse of campaign funds for personal or non-campaign use;*

3. *Withholding the truth or providing false or misleading information during appointment or other Congressional testimony except for withholding information related to national security during a public hearing or when such testimony may be covered by protections from self-incrimination or valid attorney-client privilege.*

4. *Conviction of a capital crime;*

5. *Participation in expressed or material support for insurrection or violence against a duly elected government administration or individual;*

6. *Failure to uphold the oath to defend the Constitution of the United States;*

7. *Failure by a public official or military personnel, including civilians in government service, to report to proper authority suspicion of or witnessing improper possession and/or distribution of materials that might jeopardize the security of the United States when other civilian or military justice systems fail to do so;*

8. *Any additional reason the House or Senate shall deem appropriate and make law.*

Discussion of Justification for the Changes

Pros:
Most of the reasons for including these cases are self-evident, but some are not adequately delineated in the 1787 Constitution, and the Supreme Court has issued opinions in the past that should be outside

their jurisdiction and are equivalent to making law, which the 1787 Constitution never authorized.

No list can be complete or also include all future possibilities.

Subsection 5d) Procedures for Impeachment Investigation
The House of Representatives or Senate shall, within four weeks from the date of choosing to investigate accusations for possible Impeachment, select a Special Temporary Impeachment Investigation Committee of nine of its members, four from each of the two major political parties recognized on the federal ballot and one person of another or no party affiliation chosen jointly by the leaders of the remaining minor parties on the federal ballot if no person of another or no party affiliation was elected to the House or Senate Chamber seeking Impeachment. When all Members of the Congressional Chamber involved belong to one or the other of only two parties, the ninth member shall be chosen by leaders of the two major political parties of that chamber by a two-sided coin toss. The losing party of the toss shall pick a member of the winning party to fill the ninth position.

The Special Temporary Impeachment Investigation Committee shall be limited to investigating information related to the charges for possible Impeachment.

Discussion of Justification for the Changes

Pros:
Only nine Members of the House or Senate would be needed to form such a Temporary Impeachment Investigation Committee, so both the House of Representatives and Senate would always have enough Members available for a quorum and conduct of usual business.

The number of Representatives or Senators on these committees would always be balanced if there is at least one Independent or minor-party member among the members of that chamber.

When there is no Independent or minor-party member, the ninth member would be chosen by coin flip, and the losing side would pick the ninth member from the winning side, thus taking into account a possible deliberately biased appointment to the committee.

Subsection 5e) Powers and Term of a Special Temporary Impeachment Investigation Committee.

The Special Temporary Impeachment Investigation Committee shall have power to subpoena all people serving in any federal elected or administrative office, including President, Vice-President, Cabinet Secretary or subordinate, Member of Congress, or member of the Federal Judiciary, including the Supreme Court, Federal Reserve Board, or National Redistricting Board, and any citizen believed to have significant information. Charges for impeachment investigation shall be initiated by a majority vote in the House or Senate.

1. *The subpoena power of this committee shall be enforceable for every person in the jurisdiction of the United States of America, regardless of any political office or status.*

2. *The Special Temporary Impeachment Investigation Committee shall have a six-month term to complete its investigation, from the date of acceptance of its ninth member, and submit a recommendation in writing to the full House or Senate as appropriate at the end of the investigation. Only the full House or Senate, by majority vote, shall have the power to issue Articles of Impeachment against any official of the United States government, including, but not limited to, the President, Vice President, Secretaries of the Executive Branch, justices of the Judiciary Branch, including the Supreme Court and any other federal court, or Senators and Members of the House while in office or after leaving office for offenses while in office,*

since these trials will henceforth be comparable to all other jury trials.

3. *The House of Representatives or Senate may extend the term of investigation with new limits for this Special Temporary Impeachment Investigation Committee by majority vote of all the members when the evidence gathered appears to justify an extension. There shall be no statute of limitations for these provisions because the possible impact may affect all people within the jurisdiction of the United States of America beyond the foreseeable future. The sole exceptions for terminating these proceedings shall be when there is insufficient evidence to proceed, the accused is found to be innocent by the jury, or the person has died.*

Discussion of Justification for the Changes

Pros:

A term limit for the investigation is appropriate so that the members of the committee can return to their elected responsibilities in a reasonable time and for fairness to the accused. Complicated cases may justify longer terms of investigation but must be justified so that politicians cannot use prolonging investigation as a tool to delay Committee decisions or reports. Since the subpoena powers are in this Constitution, there should be no reason for judicial appeal delays.

Subsection 5f) Sanctions for Failure to Comply with a Subpoena Regarding Impeachment Shall Be Imprisonment

Failure to appear when subpoenaed by a Committee or Subcommittee of Congress of any person when related to Constitutional violations by a public servant without justifiable medical cause for not appearing shall result in imprisonment for up to 12 months and removal from holding public office for up to one year including loss of wages and benefits while incarcerated. Imprisonment shall cease earlier if the person appears in response to the subpoena.

Such confinement shall begin one day after the date to appear and shall continue for up to one calendar year unless the subpoenaed individual submits to appear, and that person shall be released on the first day of testimony or at the end of one calendar year. Removal from office for failure to appear shall cease on the 365th day of imprisonment, or upon completion of testimony, unless the person is a target of the investigation, or cease if the charges are dismissed by the Committee or a majority vote of the full House or Senate involved.

1. *Any federal-government official shall immediately cease to exercise all duties of their position if imprisoned or Impeached, until the end of their testimony for subpoenaed witnesses, or in the case of a target, the end of the Impeachment trial, if not found guilty, and permanently if found guilty even while awaiting appeal decisions.*

2. *If a Member of the Executive or Judicial Branch is found to be guilty in a court of law and imprisoned for any reason, that individual shall cease to exercise the duties of that office and not receive any compensation related to that office until exonerated by a not-guilty verdict or hung jury. The person next in the Order of Succession shall assume the duties of the incarcerated person until charges are dismissed or sentence is completed. If the imprisoned person is found guilty of a felony related to their office, they shall be permanently removed from office and shall be ineligible to hold any public office or government employment for life.*

3. *If a Member of Congress or the Supreme Court is Impeached, that person shall immediately cease to exercise all duties of that office until found innocent or the charges are dropped by a*

51 percent vote of the Chamber of Congress that initiated the Impeachment process.

Discussion of Justification for the Changes

Pros:

The penalty for ignoring a subpoena is clearly stated, so that it can immediately be imposed.

A guilty person in jail or prison can lose their right to vote. Similarly, a person in jail or prison for ignoring a lawful federal subpoena should be denied being allowed to perform the duties of the office they occupy and all compensation related to their duties.

Subsection 5g) Method for Conducting Impeachment Trials

Impeachment trials shall be presided over by three federal judges from the nearest Court of Appeals to the site of the alleged transgressions. The Jury shall consist of twelve citizens and four alternates who reside in the State or Territory in which the most serious charges occurred, none of whom shall be a current or past public official or a political-party officer at any level or lobbyist to any level of government officials or personnel. All jury members shall be chosen under the usual procedures and rules of federal court to preside and render a verdict and prescribe the punishment if none is otherwise provided or required by federal law.

Discussion of Justification for the Changes

Pros:

Recent Impeachment trials have demonstrated that the Impeachment process delineated in the 1787 Constitution no longer works because of political divisiveness and other factors.

Citizens are tried by juries that often have twelve citizen peers and four alternates (in case one or more of the chosen is dismissed, becomes incapacitated, or dies). Not even for the most serious or heinous of crimes are juries for a trial of an ordinary citizen any larger. If no one is above the law, and all citizens are to be treated equally, then an aristocratic bias of choosing only 100 elected Senators as Impeachment jurors violates the core principle of a true democracy of equality under the law, and must be changed. When the 1787 Constitution was adopted, there were only 13 States, or 26 Senators, so the jury for an Impeachment trial was much smaller than today, but still larger than that allocated to a citizen's trial, even one charged with first-degree murder. That is not equality before the law. Furthermore, each time a new state is added, the jury for impeachment increases by two. With 100 States the jury would be 200, which is unconscionable in the context of equality. It is time to bring impeachment juries to a level of equality with other juries for serious offenses and make them less political.

Recent testimony of Supreme Court candidates at Congressional hearings have raised suspicions of less-than totally honest testimony and vetting. Having a single judge preside over an Impeachment trial, even the Chief Justice, flies in the face of minimizing prejudice or corruption in judicial proceedings. Although a three-judge panel of Appeals Court Justices does not guarantee impartiality in the court rulings, it makes it more likely, and eliminates one level of judicial appeal.

Officials in all Branches of government and levels of office must be held accountable, including judges. When officials fail to act to prevent or remove dishonorable people from government, the people should have such power. A recall procedure gives such power, as included in Section 4 above.

Subsection 5h) Prosecutors and Defendant's Attorneys in an Impeachment Trial
Prosecution shall be by attorneys from the Justice Department. Defense shall be by the defendant's chosen team of attorneys licensed to practice law

in the jurisdiction where the trial is held or by a public defender appointed by the three-judge panel presiding, when the defendant can be proven not to be able to afford legal counsel. Agreeing to be a public defender when necessary shall be a condition for being allowed to practice law in a federal court. If more than one attorney is chosen by the defendant, the defendant shall be responsible for all attorneys' fees.

Discussion of Justification for the Changes

The reasons for these provisions seem self-evident.

Subsection 5i) Compensation for Public Defenders in Impeachment Trials
Congress shall have the power to determine fair compensation for public defenders in such cases.

Discussion of Justification for the Changes

Pros:

All defendants deserve unbiased representation. Those who cannot afford to pay for such services should have assistance from the federal treasury but with safeguards against unscrupulous behavior by attorneys.

I would think that the same number of attorneys and compensation received by the Defense Department attorneys prosecuting the case would be fair, but ultimately this should be determined by Congress.

Subsection 5j) Public Contribution for Defense.
Costs of Impeachment trial defense assistance can be made by any citizen contribution not exceeding a total of $100 or more in value to all funds or individuals in public or private. This maximum amount shall change based on the national rate of inflation or deflation of the value of the

national currency. A list of the names and contributions of any donations or gifts shall be submitted to the Attorney General on a monthly basis by the defendant or the defendant's attorney until all such acitivities have ceased, in order to prevent abuse or attempts to buy favors. Donors shall not use third parties to finance or tender additional donations.

Discussion of Justification for the Changes

Pros:

Some politicians and candidates have appeared to be using campaign and other donations for judicial defense. There currently is no legal restriction on this practice of which I am aware, but I am not an attorney. There is the possibility that this practice could be used to buy political favor as a way around the Emoluments clause. Establishing a low-value limit to this practice would still allow candidates to solicit funds they may need, but small, individual donations shouldn't have enough influence to justify political favors.

Subsection 5k)

Congress shall have power to provide for this provision by appropriate legislation.

★　★　★

CHAPTER 8

Article I: Section 6: The Senate

Subsection 6a) Number, Terms, and Districts

The Senate shall be composed of an equal number of Members as the House of Representatives but never exceeding 450. Terms will be for 6 years in the Senate. The Senate districts shall be divided into three groups of as equal size as practicable so that the population represented by each Senator is as fair as possible among all the States as it is in the House of Representatives. The Federal Congressional Redistricting Board shall determine the Senate District Boundaries within 6 months after each census and whenever necessary for lawful reasons. If a State is scheduled to hold a new election because the State has lost position(s) before the term of existing Senators has expired, the longest-serving members from that state must resign on the date set for swearing-in of the new members of the Senate.

Discussion of Justification for the Changes

Table A that follows shows the distribution of seats in the House of Representatives by State (column 1), the number of Representative seats allotted to that State, based on the 2020 national census (column 2), the Average population per Representative seat in that State (column 3), the number of Senate seats allowed for that State (currently always only 2, as in (column 4), the Average Population per Senate seat (column 5) for that State, the number of seats that State would have gotten if the allocation of Senate seats had also been done by population (column 6), and gain or shortfall of Senators for that State (column 7). Even a cursory look makes it very evident that there is a great injustice in the number of Senate seats for a very large majority of the States. In a true democracy, one-person-one-vote power should dictate what that the number should be in that State instead of only two Senators per State. Population should have been the just and equal basis for Senate seats since 1787. This injustice has existed for more than 240 years and needs to be rectified, as this current Constitutional proposal will do, by making allocation of Senate seats also proportional to population and not just awarded two because of the title of being a State.

A very heated deadlock developed at the Constitutional Convention in 1787, when the smaller-population states, led by Connecticut, objected to both Houses in Congress being apportioned by population. In order to break the deadlock, Benjamin Franklin offered a compromise: each state would only have two Senators but all bills regarding spending would have to originate in the House of Representatives. Enough delegates to the convention agreed to the proposal that it passed by one vote. If you examine the table provided, it clearly shows that as more States were added, most of the States suffered a loss of power (votes) in the Senate, which greatly affected the votes in the Electoral College and the selection of Presidents. In recent history, more Presidential candidates won Electoral College victories who had actually lost the popular vote by significant margins. *Such a phenomenon is antithetical to the principle of democracy*—so much so that almost all of the new democracies that have emerged have not created Electoral Colleges but adopted direct popular vote total to choose their Presidents.

What this chart tells us is that, in most States, the people are under-represented in the Senate. After the 2020 census, because the Senate seats are still allocated only two per state to protect the interests of 6 small states, 37 other States are being denied equal representation in the Senate because of Benjamin Franklin's compromise in 1787. Does this seem equal, fair, or democratic to you?

The 21st-century Constitution rectifies this inequality by making both the House of Representatives and Senate seats based on population and the total in each house the same, so that neither chamber has an advantage over the other.

Subsection 6b) Residence Requirement for Congressional Senators
No Person shall be a Senator who shall not have attained the Age of 18 Years and been ten Years a Citizen of the United States. A person may only seek elective office to the Senate who has legally maintained continuous primary residence in that Senate district for a minimum of 10 years before the election and continue to maintain primary residence for the entire term in the Senate. "Primary residence" shall mean establishment and maintenance of a primary residence in that district for 365 days of the year. Days serving in the national capital can also count as days in the in-state primary residence.

Discussion of Justification for the Changes

Pros:

The voting age is 18, therefore, so should the minimum age to seek office, if you're old enough to understand the issues and vote, I see no justification for denying occupying the office except in cases where the candidate has not been a resident long enough to know the issues and problems in the district. Since the term of office is longer, requiring a longer residency seems reasonable.

Table A

State	Representative seats allocated*	Average Population per seat**	Senate seats allocated	Average population per Senate seat	Senate seats if allocated by population	Senate seats not allocated
Alabama	7	718,579	2	2,515,027	7	-5
Alaska	1	735,081	2	735,081	1	1
Arizona	9	795,436	2	3,579,462	9	-7
Arkansas	4	735,439	2	1,470,878	4	-2
California	52	761,091	2	19,788,366	52	-50
Colorado	8	722,771	2	2,892,084	8	-6
Connecticut	5	721,660	2	1,804,150	5	-3
Delaware	1	990,837	2	495,419	1	1
Florida	28	770,376	2	10,785,264	28	-26
Georgia	14	766,091	2	5,362,637	14	-12
Hawaii	2	730,069	2	730,069	2	0
Idaho	2	920,689	2	920,689	2	0
Illinois	17	754279	2	6,411,372	17	-15
Indiana	9	754476	2	3,395,142	9	-7
Iowa	4	798,102	2	1,596,204	4	-2
Kansas	4	735,216	2	1,470,432	4	-2
Kentucky	6	751,557	2	2,254,671	6	-4
Louisiana	6	776,911	2	2.330-733	6	-4

State	Representative seats allocated*	Average Population per seat**	Senate seats allocated	Average population per Senate seat	Senate seats if allocated by population	Senate seats not allocated
Maine	2	681,791	2	681,791	2	0
Maryland	8	773,160	2	3,092,640	8	-6
Massachusetts	9	781,497	2	3,516,737	9	-7
Michigan	13	775,726	2	5,042,29	13	-11
Minnesota	8	713,719	2	2,854,876	8	-6
Mississippi	4	740,979	2	1,481,958	4	-2
Missouri	8	770,035	2	3,080,140	8	-6
Montana	2	542,704	2	542,704	2	0
Nebraska	3	654,444	2	436,296	3	-1
Nevada	4	777,116	2	1,554,232	4	-2
New Hampshire	2	689,545	2	689,545	2	0
New Jersey	12	774,541	2	4,647,246	12	-10
New Mexico	3	706,740	2	1,060,110	3	-1
New York	26	777529	2	10,107,877	26	-24
North Carolina	14	746,711	2	5,226,077	14	-12
North Dakota	1	779,702	2	389,851	1	1
Ohio	15	787,257	2	5,904,428	15	-13
Oklahoma	5	792,703	2	1,981,758	5	-3
Oregon	6	706,917	2	2,120,751	6	-4
Pennsylvania	17	765,403	2	6,505,926	17	-15
Rhode Island	2	549,082	2	549,082	2	0
South Carolina	7	732,102	2	2,562,357	7	-5
South Dakota	1	887770	2	443,885	1	1
Tennessee	9	768,544	2	3,458,448	9	-7
Texas	38	767,981	2	14,591,639	38	-36
Utah	4	818,813	2	1,637,626	4	-2
Vermont	1	643503	2	321,752	1	1
Virginia	11	786,777	2	4,327,274	11	-9
Washington	10	771,595	2	3,857,975	10	-8

State	Representative seats allocated*	Average Population per seat**	Senate seats allocated	Average population per Senate seat	Senate seats if allocated by population	Senate seats not allocated
West Virginia	2	897,523	2	897,523	2	0
Wisconsin	8	737,184	2	2,948,736	8	-6
Wyoming	1	577,719	2	288,860	1	1
USA total	435		100		435	-335

[2] Based on U.S. Census data 2020

Subsection 6c) Phase-In of New Senators

In the first Senate election immediately after the implementation of this new Constitution, all new Senate seats shall be divided into three groups of about equal size by the President of the Senate. All Senators who have not finished their full six-year term shall remain in office until their six-year term is completed and be assigned to the appropriate group depending on the number of remaining years in their term.

The first group of Senator seats to face a new election shall be for six-year terms and include those full terms just terminated.

The second group will be for two-year terms so that the end of these terms coincide with those Senators who had two years remaining in their original terms when the change in number of seats was implemented. All of these seats will then come up for re-election at the next regular Senate election after that and be for six years.

The third group will be for four-year terms so that the end of these terms coincide with those Senators who had four years remaining in their original terms when the change in number of seats was implemented. All of these seats will then come up for re-election at the next regular Senate election after that and be for six years.

Thereafter, all seats will be subject to election on a six-year cycle except for unexpected early vacancies.

Discussion of Justification for the Changes

The details of the transition to the large number of Senators taking office need to be spelled out for legal reasons.

Subsection 6d) Redistricting after Each Census

Within six months of each ten-year census, the National Federal Election Board shall determine the federal Senate Districts for each state, which may, but do not have to exactly match, those for the House of Representatives districts.

Discussion of Justification for the Changes

This assigns duty and timing to this new entity.

Subsection 6e) Filling of Vacancies

When vacancies open in the federal Senate representation from any State, the Governor of that State shall order an election in the District represented by the vacancy, to be held within 60 calendar days of the beginning of the vacancy unless fewer than 120 calendar days remain in the term of the vacancy. All candidates seeking to be elected to fill out the remainder of the vacant term must meet age and citizenship requirements, be free of any impediments established by federal law, and register with the State office in charge of elections at least 30 days before the election.

When one or more Senate or House of Representatives seats is lost by a State because of the new Census, the longest-serving Senators and Representatives from that State must resign on the day before the opening of Congress, when the new Senators that take the seat in another State will be sworn in.

Discussion of Justification for the Changes

Procedural issue defined when a Senate seat is moved to another State because of population changes.

A mechanism for unscheduled replacements of Senate seat vacancies is required.

Subsection 6f) Temporary Offices in the Senate during Emergencies

The Vice-President of the United States shall be President of the Senate, but shall have no vote, unless the vote be equal. In the event that the Vice-President has to assume the duties of the office of President for less than 90 calendar days, the Vice-President shall nominate a successor of the same political party for Temporary Vice-President with the consent of a simple majority of the Senator of the same party to fill the position until the President is able to reassume the full duties of the office of President. When the elected President returns to fulfill the duties of the office of President, the Vice-President will return to the regular duties of that office, and the Temporary Vice-President shall resign from that office.

If the Vice-President has to assume the duties of the office of President for more than 120 days, the President shall resign, and the Temporary Vice-President shall remain in that office in the Senate until a new Vice-President is elected.

The House of Representatives and the Senate may choose to allow virtual attendance and voting at committee and general sessions, with adequate security provisions. Closed-door sessions shall be limited to items of national security, and in-person attendance shall be mandatory for all members of the subcommittee, committee, or House of Representatives or Senate involved.

Discussion of Justification for the Changes

Provides mechanism for filling of vacated positions in the Senate.

Sets minimum work terms for Senators.

The Constitution clearly needs to specify who and for how long the President of the Senate may need to be replaced. For periods exceeding 120 calendar days, the changes are discussed in **Article II, The Executive Branch.**

The terms of temporary occupancy of the offices of President and Vice President are so important that the terms of temporary occupancy or permanent replacement need to be specified in law, so that they are not abused or misinterpreted.

Section 6g) Elections

The times, types of places, and general rules for holding federal elections for all federal offices shall be prescribed by the Federal Congressional Redistricting Board for all States or by Law. The date shall be the first Monday in November and shall be a National Holiday. The choosing of election rules for federal elections such as hours, absentee ballots, voter identification, etc., shall be established by Law by the House of Representatives, Senate, and President of the United States.

Registered voters shall have the option of Absentee-voting in all fereal elctions for at least two calendar weeks before Voting Day. Individual States may grant longer periods. All such votes received within 10 days after election day shall be counted.

Discussion of Justification for the Changes

Elections controlled by the States have more frequently had rules imposed within the several States that bias, abuse, or result in hardships for the voters so as to control turnout and create hardships in that turnout. These practices are undemocratic and should have been challenged in court as being a violation of the Constitution of the United States.

Voting Day should be a National Holiday so that as many potential voters as possible are not inconvenienced or denied the right to vote. Registered voters shall have the option of Absentee voting for up to two calendar weeks before Voting Day.

Qualifications, rules, and convenience for voting have become very diverse and unequal among the States and local districts. These should be uniform for federal elections, since the right to vote in federal elections is guaranteed by the Constitution. Only Congress (by Amendment) and this Constitution will now have the authority to do so unless specified herein.

★ ★ ★

CHAPTER 9

Article I: Congress
Powers and Duties

Section 7: Powers and Duties of Congress

Subsection 7a) Attendance

Each House shall be the judge of the qualifications *and fitness of its own Members to serve. A majority must be present physically or virtually to constitute a Quorum to conduct business except that a small number may vote to adjourn, or a quorum may unanimously vote to compel all absent members to attend by a certain date unless absent because of illness.*

Absence from a session of Congress for foreign travel at taxpayer expense must be by prior legislative authorization of the travel and expenses, except when a national emergency has been declared by the President and the trip is related to the emergency declaration.

No federal money, equipment, travel, or privileges—or their equivalent—shall be used for campaign or other political purposes.

Discussion of Justification for the Changes

In the past, Treasury funds have been used for sending campaign literature and virtual messages— and even foreign propaganda—from Congressional offices. This shall no longer be allowed.

Subsection 7b) Procedures for Debate

All Members of either House, if in the chamber even virtually, shall be allowed and limited up to five minutes of debate on an individual bill and/ or amendments before any individual Member is allowed an additional five-minute period.

No Member shall be allowed to filibuster any proposed legislation, since this is an infringement on the representatives of all the other citizens' right to have their delegates' bill proposals heard and be debated.

*When proposed legislation is presented by a member of a committee or subcommittee, all members shall be given a copy of the bill or resolution and one calendar week to review the proposal. One week from the date presented, or less if the committee or subcommittee so chooses, the committee or subcommittee shall vote by roll call as to whether to debate the measure. **Committees and subcommittees must debate any issue or proposal when a majority of its members are present and vote to have such a debate scheduled.** No chairman or member shall have the power to prevent or delay such a debate without Senate or House of Representatives' approval by recorded majority vote.*

Any bill submitted to a committee or directly as a bill to the entire chamber which has at least 46 co-sponsors must be accepted for debate and vote in any committee with jurisdiction and by the entire House of Representatives or Senate during a mandated attendance ordered by the Speaker of the House of Representatives or President of the Senate. Neither the Speaker of the House nor the President of the Senate shall prevent debate of any issue in which 25% or more of those present vote to open the debate.

Otherwise, each House may determine by majority vote, the Rules of its proceedings for each session, sanctions for any of its Members for disorderly behavior while in session, and with the concurrence of two thirds of its Members, temporarily suspend or permanently expel a Member.

Discussion of Justification for the Changes

For generations, the Speaker of the House of Representatives, committee chairpersons, and other congressional leaders have had too much authority in governing what legislation is debated. All Members of Congress are elected by the People to bring forward ideas that could benefit their constituents. That is their purpose, and the leadership should not be able to block ideas because of their individual biases. These provisions give legislators additional methods to get their proposals debated in spite of leadership bias.

Each House shall keep a Journal of its actual Proceedings and only of speeches as actually delivered, when in session, and at least once each calendar month publish the same, excepting such Parts as may in their judgement require secrecy for national security reasons; and the Yeas and Nays, absent, or abstentions of each Member of either House on all votes shall be entered in the Journal.

Neither House, during the Session of Congress, shall, without the consent of the other, adjourn for more than three days, nor to any location than that in which the two Houses shall be sitting, except in an emergency wherein no other possibility exists.

Discussion of Justification for the Changes

The Journals of the House of Representative and Senate are supposed to serve as accurate reports of proceedings and votes, so that all voters can have access to the information. Printing of planned but not delivered speeches is misleading. Recording of yes and no voice votes does not tell the voters how their legislators vote. Voters have a right to this specific information every time a vote is taken.

Section 7c) Rights and Disabilities of Members

The Senators and Representatives shall receive compensation for their services, to be ascertained by law and paid out of the Treasury of the United States. They shall, in all cases, except conviction for treason, Impeachment, Felony, or Breach of Peace or Oath of Office *or arrest for a felony or physical assault or threat of assault with a weapon against any citizen, not be subject to interference* from attendance at the session of their respective Houses, and going to and returning from the same, and for any speech or debate in either House. They shall not be compelled to answer to questions in any other Place *except in response to a lawfully obtained subpoena.*

No Senator or Representative shall, during the Time for which he*/she was elected or appointed* to any civil Office under the Authority of the United States, accept any emolument current or in the future from any *private or public entity doing business with the Federal government or a State government or the military, or receive any emoluments, gifts, free travel, lodging, meals or employment, or consulting fee from any such entity, individual or group, or political candidate for a period of five years after leaving office except as specifically allowed by law.* No Person holding any Office under the United States, shall *also* be a Member of either House during his/*her* continuance in Office, except as provided herein.

Discussion of Justification for the Changes

Federal officials have been known to take or request gifts, future employment, or other rewards for themselves or others in return for political favors. Such must be unlawful to prevent corruption.

Section 8: Legislative Process, Veto Power, and Override of Supreme Court Decisions

Subsection 8a) Debt and Revenue

The debt limit must always be raised when necessary to pay for expenses of laws already enacted. All bills for raising revenue shall originate in the House of Representatives for debt payment or operation of the United States government so that it may perform its duties and pay its obligations; but the Senate may propose or concur with Amendments to the same as on other proposed legislation. All new legislation requiring spending shall contain the means of paying for the program or services without borrowing, except in national emergencies, so such legislation shall always originate in the House of Representatives.

Subsection 8b) Veto Power

Every bill which shall have passed the House of Representatives and the Senate, shall, before it becomes a law, be presented to the President of the United States; if the President approves and signs it, it shall become law, unless declared unconstitutional by the Supreme Court of the United States. But if the President shall return it to the House in which it originated unsigned, with enumeration of the Executive Branch objections and their reasons to veto, the objections and reasons shall be listed in the Journal of that House except, in cases involving National Security concerns. The House may then choose to reconsider the bill, and, if after reconsideration, two thirds by Roll Call Vote of the House shall agree to override the Presidential veto, it shall be sent again to the Senate, by which it will likewise be reconsidered, and, if two thirds of the Senate shall also agree to override the Presidential veto by Roll Call Vote, it shall become law; the names and votes of all Members of both Houses shall be published in their respective Journals for the benefit of all citizens.

If any Bill should not be returned by the President within ten days (Sundays excepted) after it is presented to him, the same shall *become the law, as if signed by the President,* unless the Congress, by adjournment before the ten-day period has occurred, prevent its return, in which case it shall not be a Law.

Every order, resolution, or vote to which concurrence may be necessary (except on the question of adjournment) shall be presented to the President of the United States, and before the same shall take effect, shall be approved by *the President,* or being disapproved by *the President,* shall *be passed* by two thirds of the Senate and House of Representatives, according to the same rules and limitations as a bill.

Subsection 8c) Override of Court Decisions

All Supreme Court Decisions shall be subject to override by the Congress, or the people, subject to the following procedures and limitations.

If a Federal Court or the Supreme Court rules that any federal law or regulation is unconstitutional, it must return the law or regulation to the Congress and, if appropriate, the Executive Branch, where it originated, with enumeration of the judiciary objections and reasons. The House or Senate, whichever originated the law involved and was the source of its intention, may then choose to reconsider the law and, after its reconsideration, two thirds by Roll Call Vote of the one House shall agree to override the Federal or Supreme Court ruling of unconstitutionality, it shall be sent to the other House, by which it will likewise be reconsidered, and, if two thirds of that House shall also agree to override the Federal or Supreme Court ruling, by Roll Call Vote, it shall become a proposed Amendment to the Constitution and sent to the States for their vote as specified in Article V.

The names and votes of all Members of both Houses and the Supreme Court members shall be published in their respective Congressional

Journals for the benefit of all citizens except in those cases involving National Security.

If one percent of the eligible voters sign a petition requesting that a Proposition be placed on the ballot of the next federal election proposing an Amendment to this Constitution, the Proposition shall be placed as soon as possible on the next federal ballot. If a simple majority of voters approve the Proposition, it shall become a Constitutional Amendment effect at 00:01 on the first day of January of the next year.

Discussion of Justification for the Changes

For more than 200 years, the Supreme Court has ruled legislation or laws, in whole or part as unconstitutional, without adequate means to override these rulings, thus enabling the courts to make law even when the majority of the public has clearly approved of the legislation, as in the case of overturning *Roe v. Wade*. The only way to overcome a Supreme Court ruling has been to write new legislation for a Constitutional Amendment; otherwise, acquiescence to the Court's demands will take place. The public has only public protest as means to try to reverse the court decision. Subsection 8c offers another new process to the public and their legislators.

Section 9: Powers of Congress

Only the National Federal Redistricting Board, with the consent of both houses of Congress, shall make the rules for election to federal offices, as specified herein, including the date, hours, types of places, and eligibility to vote. Congress may choose to delegate such duties to impartial, neutral parties at its discretion.

The Congress shall have power to lay and collect taxes, duties, imports and excises, to pay the debts and provide for the common defense and the general welfare of the United States *and its citizens and occupants,* but all *federal* taxes, duties, imports, and excises shall be uniform throughout the United States.

To borrow Money *and pay interest* on the credit of the United States *shall be mandatory; when raising the national debt ceiling to pay for money already borrowed.*

To regulate commerce with foreign nations, and among the States, *the Territories,* and *with* the *Native American* Tribes;

To establish uniform Rules *of immigration* and naturalization *for new citizens, temporary visas for travel, education, or employment,* and uniform laws on the subject of bankruptcies throughout the United States;

To *coin and print* money *or the electronic equivalent,* regulate the value thereof, and of foreign *money within the United States and its jurisdiction,* and fix the National Standard of Weights and Measures;

To provide punishment of counterfeiting the securities and current *money* of the United States *and defrauding people in the United States by foreign or domestic individuals or other entities by scams, false advertising, computer malware, or hacking of electronic devices.*

To establish Post Offices and *special communication facilities in event of threatened hostilities, domestic or foreign;*

To promote progress of science and the arts, by securing for limited times to authors and inventors, *individuals and corporations,* the exclusive right to their respective new writings, *intellectual and structural creations,* and discoveries.

To constitute federal tribunals inferior to the Supreme Court *in any location deemed necessary for protecting equal justice and a fair and timely administration of the law;*

To define and punish piracies and felonies committed *against American citizens, property, or commercial or military interests on Earth, in Space, or on any celestial body,* and offenses against the law of nations;

Discussion of Justification for the Changes

Monetary policy is up to Congress but herein is more specifically delineated.

Money (media for exchange or purchase) no longer comes as just coin but as electronic-digital entries and as unsecured currency such as Bitcoin. Such media can exist to avoid taxes, as scams, as Ponzi schemes, and totally unsecured "currency" not guaranteed by any government or other entity with required asset holdings to back the face "value." Such media of exchange should be controlled or be outlawed by the Congress for use in any transaction in or with a business entity that does business in the United States of America. To my knowledge, it currently is not thus controlled or outlawed. All profits or capital gains should also be subject to taxation if owned by Americans or U.S. corporations.

The federal government should be required to seek extradition for individuals, group members, or businesses employees foreign or domestic engaged in any fraudulent practices to cheat people within the United States or in any areas where it has jurisdiction.

(Constituitional revisions continued)

To declare war, grant letters of marque and reprisal. and make rules concerning captures;

To *exclusively* raise and support *all armed forces, including all militias except for State National Guards, local police, sheriffs, and marshals, and make appropriations of money to be used for those purposes specified in legislation for a specified period of time;*

To make rules for the government and regulation of *all federal forces bearing or not bearing arms for enforcement of federal laws or regulations*;

To provide and call forth *federal troops or other government-sanctioned* militias to execute the laws of *the United States,* suppress *domestic* insurrections and repel invasions *when the Governors of the States are unable or fail to do so in a timely manner, when more than one State is involved, or when a State requests aid from the President of the United States, or the Vice-President if the President fails to respond, or the Speaker of the House when the Executive Branch fails to respond in a timely manner.*

To provide *for organizing, arming, and disciplining militias and paying and governing them when employed in the service of the federal government,* reserving to the States respectfully the appointment of officers, the training of the members according to the discipline and level of ability prescribed by Congress.

To exercise exclusive legislation in all cases, exclusive of appropriate authority for management of city government, over the District of Columbia, and all places purchased with the consent of the legislature of the State or territory in which the same shall be located, for the establishment of *military facilities, embassies, consulates, and other needful structures for the national security,* and

To make all laws which shall be necessary and proper for carrying into execution the foregoing powers, and all other powers vested in this Constitution for the Government of the United States, or in any department or office thereof.

Discussion of Justification for the Changes

The delayed deployment of forces to deal with the Insurrection of January 6, 2021, exemplified the need in the Constitution of a Chain of Command for when local (the City of Washington did respond but did not have adequate resources to quell the insurrection), State (the District of Columbia is still not a State in spite of having all the other qualifications; several neighboring States did provide some services), Executive Branch (President Trump failed to fulfill his

Oath of Office and did not act; the Vice-President and Congressional leaders eventually had to order military intervention even though their authority to do so is not clearly delineated in the Constitution of 1787. The Constitution for the 21st century rectifies this previous lack of essential order of responsibility and authority.

Section 10: Powers Denied Congress

The Privilege of the Writ of Habeas Corpus shall not be suspended, unless, when in Cases of Rebellion or Invasion, the public safety may require it.

No Bill of Attainder or *ex post facto* law shall be passed.

No Capitation, or other direct, tax shall be laid, unless in Proportion to the Census or Enumeration herein before directed be taken.

No tax or duty shall be laid on articles **or services** exported from any State.

No preference shall be given by any regulation of commerce or revenue to the ports of one State over those of another, nor shall vessels bound to or from one State, be obliged to end, clear, or pay duties in another.

No money shall be drawn from the Treasury, but in consequences of appropriations made by law; and a regular Statement of all public Money shall be published **on at least a yearly basis.**

Discussion of Justification for the Changes

National and international services have become a large part of the American economy and should also be specified.

The need to know at least yearly of where tax and borrowed money is being spent should be a right of all Americans, since we have to pay taxes at least yearly.

(Revision of the Constitution continued)

No title of nobility shall be granted by the United States: And no person holding any office of profit or trust under them in Congress, shall, without the consent of the Congress, accept any present, emolument, office, promise of future employment, award or reward, or title, of any kind whatever, from any king, prince, or foreign State, *individual, organization, business, or corporation that engages in business with a government entity for profit, while in office or for five years after leaving office.*

Neither the House of Representatives nor the Senate shall give to its Members any financial or equivalent, insurance, or retirement benefits not already available to the average employed citizen except as specified herein.

After adoption of this Constitution, new Members of both the House of Representatives and Senate and their employees shall be allowed to participate in the Social Security Program and all other unemployment and retirement programs mandated or allowed by Congress for employed citizens of the United States, and no person shall be allowed to participate in any other financial, investment, or insurance programs limited only to federal employees.

Members of Congress retiring or not re-elected will no longer be vested for full retirement benefits for less than 20 years of service after adoption of this Constitution.

Discussion of Justification for the Changes

Neither government employees nor elected officials should be allowed to determine their own remuneration and fringe benefits except through union negotiations or oversight by an outside group of unbiased citizens. They should not be allowed to give themselves health and retirement benefits for life after only one term (currently two years for a Representative or six years for a Senator. Most workers who get even any employer-furnished benefits must work 20 to 40 years to be vested. The average American retired employee worked from starting at age 18–25 to 62–65 years of age (the prevailing Social Security retirement age when they stopped). Many continue to work after that age, because Social Security payments no longer are adequate enough to meet the rising cost of living.

When I worked for the State of California, I was told that my benefits became vested only after five years of continuous service; then they would increase by 5% per year until I retired or the benefits reached 100% at 20 years of continuous service, whichever occurred first. If I retired and later went back to State service full-time as a retired annuitant, the additional time would not change my benefits, and I would return at the lowest pay level. Why should federal service be any better?

Politicians and government officials and employees should not have special privileges in a democracy. Some citizens should not be more equal than others.

Section 11. Powers Denied to the States

No State shall enter into any treaty, alliance, or confederation; grant letters of marque and reprisal; coin or print *money*; emit bills of credit; make any thing but gold and silver coin *or lawful money* of the United States as tender in payment of debts; pass any bill of attainder, *ex post facto* law, or law impairing the obligation of contract, or grant any title of nobility *or special privilege*.

No State shall, without the consent of the Congress, lay any imposts or duties on imports or exports, except what may be absolutely necessary for executing its inspection laws; and the net produce of all duties and imposts, laid by any State on imports and exports, shall be for the use of the Treasury of the United States; all such laws shall be subject to revision and control by the Congress.

No State shall, without the consent of Congress, lay any duty of tonnage, keep troops, ships, *or other weapons or equipment* of war or *militias* in times of peace without the specific consent of Congress, enter into any agreement or compact with another State, or with a foreign power, or engage in war, unless actually invaded, or in such imminent danger as not to admit for delay

★ ★ ★

Article II: Section 1: The President

The executive power shall be vested in a President of the United States.

He shall hold his Office during the Term of four Years, together with the Vice-President *of the same political party, be chosen for the same Term, and both* be elected as follows:

The United States, striving to be a Democracy of, by and for the People, the direct vote of the People in each State and Territory of the United States of America who have reached the age of eighteen years on or before election day of that year shall be counted for federal offices without interference by any individual, organization, or agency. The governor or chief executive of that State or Territory shall make a list of all persons voted for, and the number of votes for each; which list they shall sign, certify, and seal in the presence of Members of the ruling bodies of that State or Territory, and transmit to the seat of government of the United States, directed to the President of the Senate. In the event that the governor of a State, or chief executive of a Territory, or the President of the Senate is incapacitated, the person who is next in the line of succession for that office, and available, shall assume those duties, and, in signing the list shall note why they were made responsible for signing or supervising the counting of the votes.

The President of the Senate, or required substitute, shall, in the presence of Members of the Senate and House of Representatives, open all the legitimate certificates, and the votes shall be counted. The person having the greatest number of votes of the citizens shall be the President-elect, to take the Oath of Office at noon on the next Inauguration Day. The person running with the President-elect for the office of Vice-President shall be the Vice-President-Elect.

No person except a natural-born Citizen of the United States *who has attained to the age of thirty-five years and has been a continuous resident within the United States or one of its Territories, except those who have been otherwise assigned or ordered by an agency or official of the United States government, for official duties, such as ambassadors, embassy employees,* et al., *to temporarily serve outside the United States, shall be eligible for the Office of President or Vice-President.*

No federal official, including the President and Vice-President, shall be immune from indictment, trial while in office, or serving any sentence imposed by criminal or impeachment trial after removal from office, because of their conviction, since a Constitutional provision now exists for their replacement.

In case of the removal of the President from Office due to death, or imprisonment or a guilty verdict after impeachment or a Federal or State felony trial, resignation, inability to discharge the power and duties of the Office, the Office and duties of the President shall pass to the Vice-President to finish the Term.

When the Vice-President is required to replace the President, or the Vice-President is no longer able to perform the duties of that office as determined by a vote in the Senate of members of the same political party, an emergency national election shall be held within 90 days to elect a new Vice-President from candidates of the same political party.

The candidate receiving the most votes, even if not a majority, shall take the oath of office and assume the duties within one week after the election.

The President and Vice-President shall receive, at stated times, for the services of their respective offices, a compensation, which shall be neither increased nor diminished during the term for which either shall have been elected. Any emolument, gift, or service received by either person of greater than $100 while in either office shall be the property of the People of the United States and remain with the government when that person leaves office. Failure to do so shall be an impeachable offense.

Before the President, Vice President, or any federal officer assumes the duties of their office, they shall take the following oath of office, whenever possible covered live by public media or before an assembly of the American People, and other public officials:

"I (the name of the person), do solemnly swear (or affirm) that I will faithfully execute the office of the President of the United States, (or the Office they are about to assume), and will to the best of my ability preserve, protect and defend the Constitution of the United States with malice toward none and for the equal benefit of all."

Discussion of Justification for the Changes

In recent history a Vice-President was forced to resign (Spiro Agnew), and the President appointed a successor (Gerald Ford) under the terms of the 1787 Constitution. Subsequently, the President (Richard Nixon) resigned rather than face impeachment, and a person (Gerald Ford) not elected by the People became President. No one should be able to become President without the vote of the people in a democracy. This situation could have resulted in a person becoming President with a very different agenda than either of those elected by the people. As it was, President Ford pardoned Richard Nixon for his wrongdoing while in office so that he would not face criminal charges. This was a bad precedent, and these circumstances should never be repeated.

A new President or Vice-President replacing a person unable to finish a term in the same office for any reason should be of the same political party to minimize major changes in policy between regular Presidential elections.

Since the President and Vice-President elected are from the same political party, any replacement of either position should also be of that party until the next election for these offices. Under the new rules and procedures of this Constitution, impeachment trials will no longer be performed in the Senate but in front of a common jury of citizen peers. Since these trials will be in regular courts of law, the judge and jury will have authority to impose criminal and civil penalties if warranted for any crimes for which the defendant is found guilty by the jury.

Section 2: Powers of the President

The President shall be Commander-in-Chief of *all the armed forces* of the United States, and the militia of *all* the states, when called into the actual service of the United States; the President may require the opinion, in writing, of the principal officer in each of the Executive Departments, upon any subject relating to the duties of their respective offices.

The President shall have the Power:

By and with the advice and consent of the Senate, to make Treaties, *with the Senate voting on the proposal within 3 months of its submission to the Senate by the President, and it shall be approved, provided two thirds of the Senators present concur when a quorum is present;*

Nominate, and by and with the Advice and Consent of the Senate, shall appoint qualified ambassadors, other public ministers and consul, judges of the Supreme Court, federal judges, officers of federal departments and agencies and all other Officers of the United States whose appointments are not herein otherwise provided for and which shall be established by law, but Congress, may, by law, vest the appointment of such inferior officers, as they think proper, in the President alone or in the heads of departments. If a vacancy opens in any of these positions, the President must nominate a replacement within a month, and the Senate must vote on the nominee within two months of the nomination as long as the required vote occurs before the President has left office.

Nominations by the President authorized by this Constitution shall be debated within the Senate within 30 calendar days. No delays may be imposed by Congress or any government employee or elected official except the President when the President is acting within the authority of the office. If the debate or a vote does not occur within 30 calendar days of the nomination, the nominations for whom there has not been a vote shall be considered as accepted by all and be appointed except during a recess of the Senate when the counting of the days shall be suspended until the Senate reconvenes to the offices specified.

After proper vetting for qualifications and ethical standards, such nominees shall require the approval of a majority of a quorum of Senators excepted as otherwise provided.

The President shall have the Power to *temporarily* fill all vacancies that may open during the Recess of the Senate, by granting Commissions *which shall expire when the Senators reconvene and vote on the permanent replacements submitted by the President within one week of the commencement of that Senate session.*

The President shall have the Power to delegate duties to the Vice-President for specified durations during the term in office.

Discussion of Justification for the Changes

A new improper tactic has emerged in the 21st century—of presidential nominations being blocked by not being vetted, debated, or voted upon for a year before the Presidential term has expired. This may have been technically legal but clearly violated the spirit of the 1787 Constitution. The new Constitution will clearly make such tactics illegal.

Temporary appointments have been misused in recent decades, and, so, a time limit needs to be specified so that Congress can vote on these appointments as soon as it reconvenes.

Section 3: Additional Duties of the President

The President shall:

At least once per year, give to Congress information *regarding* the State of the Union, and recommend to their consideration such *measures and goals as the President shall judge necessary and expedient to advance the welfare, safety and national security of the citizens and United States;*

May, on extraordinary occasions or national emergencies or disasters, request in writing the convening of one or both Houses of Congress for advice and making of laws to alleviate or assist in restoring the welfare of the citizens impacted;

In cases of disagreement between the Houses with respect to the time of adjournment, the President may adjourn them to such time as may be proper;

Receive ambassadors and other public ministers;

Negotiate the release or exchange of Americans imprisoned in other countries;

Take care that all federal laws be faithfully and properly executed;

Commission all officers of the United States *and its armed forces and militias, with the advice and consent of the Senate within 30 days of the Presidential approval except during Senate recess when the counting of days shall be suspended until the Senate reconvenes; the nominee shall be considered accepted by all as appointed to the office and rank specified.*

May, on extraordinary occasions or national emergencies or disasters, request in writing the convening of the Supreme Court for a special session in order to consider and rule on an issue requiring the immediate attention of that Court.

Discussion of Justification for the Changes

Recent decades have demonstrated an accelerating rate of change and crises. The three Branches of Government must be able to consult each other's advice during recesses when emergencies occur. This is now clearly authorized for the President in this Constitution for the 21st century.

Section 4: Removal from Office

The President, Vice President, and all civil officers of the United States, shall be removed from office *on conviction by a jury of citizens of an Impeachable offense, treason or espionage during time of peace or hostilities,* bribery, *failure to report emoluments,* or high crimes *or felonies, and be barred for life from any public office or position of public trust.*

Discussion of Justification for the Changes

Pros:
People who have been found guilty of such offenses should not be trusted in public office.

Section 5: Powers Not Given to the President

The President shall not have the power to pardon persons accused or convicted of any crime, since the proper venue for judicial decisions shall be in the powers of Article III.

The President shall not use the military or militias within the borders of the United States except when asked to do so by the Governor of a State or Territory or to stop violence or insurrection when a State Executive appears to be unwilling or unable to do so. Whenever possible, the President should do so with the advice and consent of the Senate, unless time is of the essence to save lives, as determined by the Joint Chiefs of Staff.

Discussion of Justification for the Changes

For a single person in any form of government to have pardoning power for any crime is an invitation for corruption and must be abolished.

★　★　★

CHAPTER 11

Article III: Section 1: Structure of the Judicial Branch

Subsection 1a) Appointment, Term, and Age

The judicial Power of the United States shall be vested in one Supreme Court, and in such *lower* Courts as the Congress may from time to time establish *by law*.

All federal judges, including the Supreme Court, shall serve a term of not more than ten years unless renominated by the President and reconfirmed by the Senate. Terms shall last only until a judge reaches 70 years of age unless renominated and confirmed. Any justices currently serving on a federal court bench who has or will attain the age of 69 must tender their resignation to the President on their 70th birthday. Each judge must then be renominated or replaced by the President with the concurrence of Congress by roll call vote. Judges older than age 70 shall be subject to renomination and reconfirmation on a yearly basis thereafter. More than one lower court judge may be nominated and voted on simultaneously, unless 10 or more Senators object in writing to the President to one or more choices. These choices must then be withdrawn or considered individually by a quorum of the Senate.

The Supreme Court shall consist of nine judges nominated by the President and approved by a two-thirds majority of those present during a quorum of the Senate within 60 days of the nominations. One year after the adoption of this Constitution, any federal judge serving shall resign, including Supreme Court justices, if older than age 70. New judges may begin the new ten-year term as soon as the Senate approves the nomination. At least six months before each new term is to begin, the President must submit the three nominees after proper vetting in the order of preference for each vacant Supreme Court position. If all three nominees are rejected, the President shall nominate three more until all vacant positions are filled and as needed thereafter.

Judges for lower courts may be selected in a group, which the Senate shall accept or reject as a group or individually within 3 months. Nominees will be submitted to the Senate until all vacant positions are filled and as needed thereafter.

A judge already in the position may be renominated for another term.

Discussion of Justification for the Changes

Terms for judges were made lifetime appointment in the 1787 Constitution with the intent of preventing bias or political pressures from affecting judicial decisions. Appointments are currently made by the President, and outside political groups have been getting undue influence on the types of judges dominating the judicial system. A small Senate vote majority resulted in blocking a previous nomination for over a year until that President left office.

Federal judges, especially the Supreme Court, are currently not chosen by the People but by politicians (outside groups that make recommendations to the President and to a Senate which are heavily weighted to favor the smaller, more-conservative rural populations over the more populous States with a larger urban/liberal citizenry. Current restriction of only two Senators per State has denied equal representation for citizens in the Senate.

Recent appointments have often shown political or religious bias and even withholding vital vetting information, poor vetting-investigation quality, influence by political organizations of wealthy individuals trying to protect their self-interests, which violates the necessity for honesty, open-mindedness, the Will of the People and the fundamental one-person-one-vote premise of a true democracy, and permits hidden agendas. This must be stopped.

With a large Senate, the will of the whole population is more likely to affect the final appointments, which is what is supposed to happen in a democracy.

Term limits for justices are more likely to allow changes in political philosophy in our legal structure as the political desires of the citizenry change, another precept that is fundamental to a true democracy. The assumption that lifetime appointments would decrease bias and corruption have proven to be false. Term limits also promote removal of justices whose mental acuteness or knowledge of recent changes in law may make their continuance on the bench suspect or undesirable to the people.

Terms of judges should not last automatically past 69 years of age, but a judge deemed to still be capable of fulfilling the office may be renominated on a yearly basis until there is question of ability by the President or the Senate. To expect all older justices to recognize the onset of their own senility or deteriorating ability is foolish, so lifetime terms until a judge resigns is an invitation to a deteriorating justice system. Some older individuals remain very cognitively skilled, so age alone should not mean automatic exclusion for all based solely on age.

Although age limitations for Congress may seem justified, Members of Congress are chosen directly by the people and decisions about age and fitness should be left to the People in a democracy. Term limits are unnecessary and can remove valuable experienced individuals when term durations requiring reelection and recall provisions exist.

Subsection 1b) Behavior, Reports, Recusing

All federal judges, both of the Supreme *Court* and *lower* courts, including the Chief Justice, shall hold their offices during good behavior *free of scandal, bribes, acceptance of emoluments of greater than $100 in value, or conviction of felonies, racial, sexual, religious, ethnic or national discrimination for a period of ten years. Each judge shall file an annual written report of all gifts totaling more than $100, and property financial transactions of more than $5,000 received by the judge, the spouse, any dependents, household members, or from any person, organization, political entity, business, or equivalent in services, political advertising in any form of media, or to any of those listed. Supreme Court Judges shall submit the report to the appropriate judicial oversight committee in Congress. Lower-court federal judges shall send the report to the court at the next highest level of the judicial system by April 15 of the succeeding calendar year.*

All federal judges must recuse themselves from any proceeding in which they, a relative, or business partner has any financial or political involvement.

Failure to comply, except for serious illness, shall be cause for immediate resignation, impeachment, or dismissal.

Discussion of Justification for the Changes

Unfortunately, recent events have exposed sufficient lapses in honesty and ethics that it is now necessary to include ethical criteria in this constitutional proposal.

Subsection 1c) Compensation and Retirement

Judges, both of the Supreme and Lower Federal Courts, shall at a stated time, receive for their services a compensation, which shall not be diminished during their continuance in office. Each judge shall also receive Social Security Retirement payments for service upon reaching the age authorized for others to begin receiving Social Security Retirement payments if enrolled and meeting all Social Security criteria upon reaching the age authorized for others to begin receiving Social Security Retirement payments. The amount of retirement compensation for a judge shall be 1.25% of base pay for each 6 months served as a federal judge up to but not exceeding 100% of the highest base payment while in active service.

Congress shall have the power to change or amend these provisions by law or amendment.

Discussion of Justification for the Changes

Retirement compensation for working Americans has become more tenuous. Government employees at all levels should not get full benefits for short-term employment. Level of benefits should reflect levels of and duration of public service.

Section 2: Powers of the Judicial Branch

Subsection 2a) Ruling on the Constitutionality of American Laws

The Supreme Court shall have *jurisdiction in cases involving the constitutionality of any State or Federal Law. States, or State Courts, may not pass or enforce any law expanding, diminishing, attempting to interpret, or in violation of the Federal Constitution.*

Subsection 2b) Limitations on Interpretation and Duty to Report Unconstitutionality to Congress.

The intent of Federal Laws initiated in and passed by both houses of Congress can be best known by the members of Congress that made the law. If the law is declared unconstitutional by any federal court, that court shall notify both Houses of Congress and the President of all parts of a law it believes are unconstitutional, the reasons and issues, and any corrective actions that are necessary in its opinion. Congress may intercede at this or any level of the federal legal system or wait for a final Supreme Court decision.

This does not empower the courts at any level to make law by declaring parts of any law or case precedent as equal to a new law; that is the sole power of Congress.

Discussion of Justification for the Changes

The Supreme Court has been making law for centuries, using its ability to make laws unconstitutional. When it began making parts of laws constitutional, it began actually making new laws by essentially amending laws by declaring only parts unconstitutional. This power was never given to the court system in the Constitution of 1787. This 21st-century Constitution clearly denies the court system the right to amend or change any law. The sole authority the courts have is to state that a law is constitutional or not. A law means *the entire law.* It can act in an advisory capacity by advising what part of a law is questionable and how that might be rectified but not to change the law, which it has been doing unchallenged. The new Constitution fixes this problem.

Subsection 2c) Disputed Constitutionality Cases Can Become Amendments
The Congress can dispute a decision by the Supreme Court by amending and passing the amended law or by submitting the law to a two-thirds majority vote in both Houses and as a Constitutional Amendment directly to the States. If the law is favored by two thirds of the legislatures of the several States within two years, it shall become a Constitutional Amendment. If not approved by the several States within two years, it shall be placed on the ballot of the next national election. If a majority of voters approve of the measure in the national election, it shall become a

valid Amendment to the Constitution, since, in a true democracy, rules are ultimately determined by the will of the People they govern.

Discussion of Justification for the Changes

Many states have a Proposition format, whereby the citizens can amend the State Constitution by a majority vote, making the Proposition an amendment to the State Constitution. It is time that the national Constitution have a means for the Congress and the President to override the opinion of nine people on the Supreme Court or for the population of voters to override it. Section 2c creates that power and restores balance of power not only to the Congress and President but, more importantly, to the People directly.

Subsection 2d) Court Decisions Do Not Become Case-Precedent Law
Case-precedent decisions in any court case shall apply only to the case in question and may not be used as justification for other cases, which must be judged on their own merits, unless new Federal or State laws are enacted to encode the case precedent as law. This Constitution does not give the power to make law to any single person, any judge, including the appeals courts or even the Supreme Court; it is a sole prerogative and duty of Congress.

Discussion of Justification for the Changes

From the beginning, the courts have been making law by case precedent, as was done under old English Common Law, in the days before Constitutional law. Only Congress and the Amendment process can give lawmaking power to the ancient common-law court practice. There is no provision in the 1787 Constitution that spells out such a power for the courts.

Subsection 2e) Constitutionality of Treaties, Cases of Admiralty or Maritime Jurisdiction

Where the decision may be interpreted as a new law, the Supreme Court shall have the power to review the constitutionality of treaties and cases of Admiralty and Maritime Jurisdiction to which the United States may be a party.

Subsection 2f) Controversies Between States, or States and Foreign Entities and United States Citizens

The Supreme Court or a lower federal court shall have sole jurisdiction in resolving controversies between States; between a State and one or more citizens of another State; between citizens of the same State claiming lands, other real property, or goods in a different State; or between a citizen or citizens and a foreign government, entity, citizens, or subjects.

Subsection 2g) Other Duties of the Supreme Court

In all cases of foreign ambassadors, other public ministers and consuls, and those to which a State shall be a party, the Supreme Court shall have original jurisdiction. In all other cases, the Supreme Court shall have appellate jurisdiction, both as to law and fact, with such exceptions and under such regulations as Congress shall make.

Subsection 2h) Other Trials and Impeachments

The trials for all crimes, *including* cases of impeachment, shall be by jury. Such trials shall be held in the *judicial district* where the *alleged* crimes shall have been committed; when not committed within any State, the trial shall be at such place or places as the Congress may by law *direct or* have directed.

Discussion of Justification for the Changes

Except for politicians and judges, all crimes by ordinary people—both citizens and non-citizens—shall be tried by a jury of up to 12 peers. Only trial by a Senate of 100 members (which increases by two more each time a new State is added) does a special pseudo-aristocracy called "politicians and judges" get an impossible jury of biased individuals. It is at least a century overdue that this inequity be fixed. Article III Subsection 2h does so.

★ ★ ★

CHAPTER 12

Article III:
Section 3: Treason

Section 3: Treason

Treason against the United States shall consist in *levying war or insurrection against the lawful government, or to spying or espionage for, giving aid or comfort, or propaganda assistance to an enemy of the United States during peace or war. No person shall be convicted of treason unless on the testimony of two witnesses to the overt act, confession in open court, or electronic, photographic, or video recording of the act. A person may face treason and espionage charges at the same time.*

The Congress shall have the Power to declare the punishment of treason *if other than life imprisonment without pardon or parole, and no person shall be tried for treason except during the life of the person.*

Discussion of Justification for the Changes

Webster's New World Dictionary declares "treason against the United States shall consist only in levying war against them, or in adhering to their enemies, giving them aid and comfort." Many have interpreted this as treason can only occur in times of declared war. The placement of the comma and the word "or" after the first phrase can also mean that what follows are additional conditions in which one commits treason besides war: "in adhering to their enemies, giving them aid and comfort" are two additional means of committing treason.

Citizens of the United States suffer loss of life, imprisonment, torture, and suffering because others have given aid and comfort to an enemy when there is no declaration of war or even non-violent hostilities. If this is not treason, what is it?

★　★　★

CHAPTER 13

Article IV:
Relations Between the States

Section 1: All States Shall Accept Judicial Decisions in Other States

Full faith and credit shall be given in each State *and Territory* to the public acts, records, and judicial proceedings of every other State *and Territory under federal jurisdiction. Congress* may, by general laws, prescribe the manner in which such acts, records, and proceedings shall be proved and the effect thereof.

Section 2: Extradition

The citizens of each State and Territory under federal jurisdiction shall be entitled to all privileges and immunities of the citizens in the States and Territories under federal jurisdiction.

A person charged in any State with treason, felony, or other crime, who shall flee from justice and be found in another State, shall, on demand of the Executive Authority of the State from which he fled, be delivered up, *and* be removed to the State having jurisdiction over the crime *for a trial to be held within one year from the date surrendered and, if found innocent, shall be immediately released.*

No person held for service, imprisonment, or labor in one State as punishment being found guilty in a court of Law, shall, in consequence of any law or regulation therein, be discharged from such service, imprisonment, or labor, but shall be delivered up *and be removed to the State having jurisdiction over the crime.*

Discussion of Justification for the Changes

Article IV, Section 2 is to ensure that the various States honor each other's obligations to extradite people in their jurisdiction who have violated laws in another State.

Section 3: Formation and Admission of New States

New States may be admitted by the Congress into this Union, but no new State shall be formed or erected within the jurisdiction of any other State; no State may be formed by the junction of two or more states or parts of States, without the consent of the legislatures of the States *and three quarters of the citizens of voting age* concerned as well as *the roll-call vote of three quarters of both Houses of* Congress.

The Congress shall have the Power to dispose of and make all needful rules and regulations respecting the Territories or other property belonging to the United States; nothing in this Constitution shall be so construed as to prejudice any claims of the United States or of any particular State.

Section 4: Federal Responsibility to the States

The United States shall guarantee to every State in this Union a *Democratic* Republican form of government, shall protect each of them against invasion, and, on application of the legislature or the executive when the legislature cannot be convened *in sufficient time against domestic violence.*

Discussion of Justification for the Changes

Taking territory from one State for the purpose of creating or changing the borders of another should not require just the votes of politicians, but, because it can be very disruptive to the well-being and pursuit of happiness of individual citizens, it should also require the overwhelming consent of those of voting age.

We must emphasize that the goal of this change is to establish a more perfect democracy.

★　★　★

CHAPTER 14

Article IV:
Section 5: Withdrawal or Removal of a State from the Union

Since States have been admitted to the Union by request and consent of the territory and citizens thereof, and with the consent of the legislatures of the States concerned, as well as of Congress, and in order to allow the peaceful withdrawal or removal of a State and its willing citizens to sever all relations, rights, responsibilities, and benefits of membership in the United States of America, a State or territory may do so on the first day of the following calendar year if 12 or more months intervene from the date of the submission of the request to withdraw, and if all of the following conditions are met:

   a. *The Executive and three quarters of both Houses of the State or Territory's legislature wishing to depart must, by roll-call vote, petition the Congress of the United States to do so;*

b. *At least three quarters of citizens of federal voting age must, in a free and fair election, agree to the petition before it is submitted to Congress;*

c. *All citizens wishing to depart the State before or after it secedes must be given the opportunity to freely do so, taking whatever possessions they own with them;*

d. *All citizens choosing to depart must be paid fair compensation as determined by a federal court of the United States for any real property or possession they are unable to remove when they depart;*

e. *The State shall surrender to the United States all equipment and weapons of war within that State and pay fair compensation to the United States Treasury, as determined by a Federal Court of the United States, for all federal property and equipment that cannot be removed by the federal government, including but not limited to, known mineral rights and natural resources on federal lands, national parks, buildings and structures, roads, dams, power-generating, -storage, and -transmission structures and equipment, and bridges, except for any paid for entirely with State funds.*

f. *Both Houses of Congress shall agree to all terms and conditions of the withdrawal by a roll-call vote of approval by three quarters of the members of both Houses excepting and not counting the current Members of both Houses representing the State seeking removal in any of the calculations or votes.*

g. *Congress may remove any State that participates in insurrection or seeks to undermine any lawful and free federal election by a three-quarters vote of approval by the Members of both Houses and impose any or all of the conditions in Section 5 above.*

Discussion of Justification for the Changes

The original States joined the United States voluntarily. Most of the States since also asked to be members, even the Republic of Texas.

The Constitution of 1787 provides no peaceful method for a State to request and be granted separation or to be expelled. The result, from 1860 to 1865, was the bloodiest, deadliest, and most disruptive war in American history, wherein Americans fought, killed, and destroyed the families and property of other Americans who wanted to leave and form a different country.

The war was fought over many issues: slavery, States' rights, and ownership of federal facilities. This war, in many ways, continues even now, with violence, vigilante and guerrilla war tactics, illegal gangs with caches of weapons of war, and even fascist goals for some.

Lincoln hesitated to call forth federal troops when States began to secede because the Constitution did not address such a possibility or provide a mechanism for or against it. When South Carolina troops fired on Fort Sumter, Lincoln used their successful attempt to seize federal property which the State considered to be theirs, as the reason for calling troops to action.

A modern Constitution should provide lawful and peaceful methods to withdraw but with compensation to the United States for the infrastructure and resource development paid for with federal taxes paid by the citizens of all the States, including return to the federal government of military equipment and weapons and the cost of military facilities that it will have to abandon.

These are reasonable demands, which any State or Territory should reimburse to the citizens who remain in the Union.

I would personally prefer that all States choose to remain since their chance of maintaining independence, prosperity, democracy, the highest general welfare, and equal justice still would best remain as part of the Union, but giving them the option demonstrates that they are not being held hostage.

★　★　★

CHAPTER 15

Article V:
Amending This Constitution

The Congress, whenever two thirds of both Houses shall deem it necessary, shall propose Amendments to this Constitution, or on the application of the legislatures of two thirds of the several States, shall call a Convention for proposing Amendments, which, in either case, shall be valid to all intents and purposes, as part of this Constitution, when ratified by the legislatures of three fourths of the several States, or by Conventions in three fourths thereof, as one or the other mode of ratification may be proposed by the Congress. If one percent of the registered voters sign a petition to put a Proposition for a Constitutional Amendment and present it to the President of the Senate, the Proposition shall be placed on the ballot of the next federal election and if passed by a simple majority of votes, it shall become an Amendment to this Constitution and become effective at 00:01 on the first day of January of the next calendar year.

Article VI: Debts, Treaties, and Existing Laws

All debts contracted and engagements entered into, before the adoption of this Constitution, shall be as valid against the United States under this Constitution, as under the *previous Constitution.*

This Constitution, the laws of the United States which shall be made pursuant thereof, *and all Treaties* made or which shall be made, under the Authority of the United States, shall be the Supreme Law of the Land. *The Supreme Court and* the judges in every State shall be bound thereby, *unless declared unconstitutional by the Supreme Court and not overturned by Congress or a plebiscite of the people,* anything in the Constitution or laws of any State to the contrary notwithstanding.

The aforementioned Senators and Representatives, the Members of the State legislatures, and executives and judicial officers, both of the United States and of the several States, shall be bound by the Oath of Affirmation, to support this Constitution. *Failure to do so may be subject to impeachment investigation by a twelve-member committee by either House of Congress or State legislature acting as a Grand Jury, with subpoena and investigative authority, and, by majority vote, referral to a Federal or State court of law, as appropriate, for a trial by jury of twelve citizens and four alternates of voting age. Conviction by unanimous vote shall result in immediate dismissal from office, possible incarceration, parole, or fines.*

Discussion of Justification for the Changes

The Congress and State legislatures will have the power to impeach their officials who violate Federal or State law or their respective oath of office, and both will be able to refer the case to a jury of citizens if the several States also opt to use trial by jury.

Discussion of Justification for the Changes

The final decision in a democracy should always remain with the people.

★　★　★

Article VII:
Ratification of the Modern Constitution
for the 21st Century

The ratification of *three quarters of the existing State legislatures shall be sufficient* for the establishment of this Constitution between the existing States, *or, if ratification has not occurred by the next national election, the measure shall be placed on the ballot as a Proposition measure to adopt this Amendment to this Constitution by a simple majority of the voting citizens in a national plebiscite as delineated in Article V.*

Discussion of Justification for the Changes

The final decision in a democracy should always remain with the people.

★ ★ ★

Article VIII:
Bill of Rights of all Citizens
and Permanent Residents

Subsection 1a) Freedom of Religion

Neither Congress *nor any State* shall make any law with respect to an establishment of religion or the expression or exercise thereof, or of religious free speech except if it impinges on the freedom of others, advocates commission of a crime or violence toward others or any institution of government. *There shall be no nationally endorsed religion in the United States. No religious test shall ever be required as a qualification for any office or public trust under the United States or any State.*

Discussion of Justification for the Changes

There have been a few politicians and others advocating that the United States should declare itself a Christian nation. This would be a violation of all Americans' basic democratic rights and make them second-class citizens in a country that professes the equality of all. It would be hypocrisy, plain and simple.

Subsection 1b) Freedom of Speech

Neither Congress nor any State shall make *any* law respecting *freedom of expression of political or any other views or opinions, provided that they are not false or are verifiable as true. Congress shall be empowered to make any necessary laws to prevent the dissemination of unverifiable propaganda, rumors, exaggerations, conspiracy theories, advertisements, or videos, recordings, or speeches containing known falsehoods that can damage or destroy a person's or institution's reputation or hinder someone's ability to pursue happiness—or even get a fair trial.*

Subsection 1c) Freedom of the Press and Media

Neither Congress nor any State shall make *any* law respecting *printed, broadcast, or recorded media with regard to freedom of expression or views except for disseminating unlawful propagandizing information, images, or altered communications known to be false, reports or rumors damaging to the reputation of any person or entity unless verifiable as true, and pictures or graphics violating privacy without signed permission of every person in the material unless more than six people are easily identifiable. Recording the material for possible evidence of an unlawful act is permitted.*

Discussion of Justification for the Changes

Free, truthful speech is critical in a democracy, but unrestrained speech to damage or destroy another person or entity or bias a judge or jury is abuse and misinterpretation of what is meant by free speech, a free press, and free media. Those things forbidden above can easily become grounds for litigation, but, by then, the damage may have already been done to a person or organization that is not reparable with monetary awards.

If more than six people are in a picture, graphic, or video, it can be an unreasonable requirement to get signed permission from every identifiable person in the material. Recording of possibly unlawful acts should always be legal because of their potential evidentiary value.

Subsection 1d) Freedom of Assembly

Neither Congress nor any State shall make any law respecting freedom of assembly *except in areas that compromise public safety or freedom of travel and inside public facilities where documents pertaining to national security may be stored or in use, or if the assembly advocates violence against any persons or public institutions.*

Discussion of Justification for the Changes

Freedom of assembly is essential for peaceful, positive protest and expression of grievances. Use of violence cancels any pretense of peaceful assembly or protest and violates the rights of the innocent.

Subsection 1e) Freedom of Petition

Neither Congress nor any State shall make any law with respect to peaceful freedom of petition of grievances or outlawing any political party or movement unless it advocates or encourages violent change in the government or any of its institutions.

Subsection 1f) Right to Bear Arms

Weapons of war deemed by Congress to be necessary for national security and safety shall be regulated and limited to military, law enforcement, National Guard, and other personnel necessary for public safety or national security. A militia of the People, well-regulated by the government of the People, being necessary to the security of a free State, the right of the People to keep and bear *arms for self-protection and sport* shall not be infringed *except to prevent unlawful harm to other citizens or commission of criminal acts.*

Congress shall have the authority to make such laws governing the ownership, licensing, storage, and use of arms for self-protection and sport.

Discussion of Justification for the Changes

Weapons of war cannot be justified for personal protection, hunting, or sport. Their purpose is for war against an enemy external or internal. "Internal enemy" implies insurrection, which could lead to destruction of our democracy. Current interpretations by many people imply that I can own weapons for war—even armored vehicles, weaponized drones, military-grade aircraft, guided missiles, and nuclear weapons. Such ability will lead to chaos and even heightened fear everywhere we go. This will lead to a fortress mentality and loss of all security and freedom. The right to bear arms needs better definition and protections for all people.

Many people, lobbies, manufacturers, and marketers will oppose these limitations, but the rights of most people to freedom of movement and freedom from fear are more important than forming private, illegal armies against imagined government abuse or invasion. If people are so afraid of our government, perhaps a better alternative is for them to find some other country to which they should move, if they can find one, take all their weapons with them, and see if that country will allow them to purchase, own, and brandish weapons of war.

Subsection 1g) Housing of Military and Law Enforcement Personnel

No military, *law-enforcement, or militia personnel* shall be quartered in any house *during peace or war* without the consent of the owner, and then only in a manner to be prescribed by Law.

Subsection 1h) Citizen Rights to Privacy, Security, and Unreasonable Searches and Seizures

The right of the People to be secure in their persons, *privacy of information,* houses, papers, and effects from searches, seizures, *or dissemination without written permission,* shall not be violated, and no warrants be issued, except upon probable cause, supported by oath or affirmation, and, particularly, describing the place to be searched, the persons or things to be seized, or *information to be released and compelling reason to do so.*

Subsection 1i) Self-Incrimination

Military personnel charged with a crime related to military service shall be tried by Court Martial, according to the Laws of the Military Code of Conduct and its laws and regulations. No military personnel or their legal partner shall be forced to testify against themselves or their domestic partner.

No person shall be held to answer for a capital or otherwise infamous crime, unless on a presentation or indictment of a Grand Jury, regardless of present position or duties, but such an indictment shall be enforceable even against *the President, Vice-President, Cabinet Members, Ambassadors, or Members of Congress, all of whom shall be subject to indictment and trial while in office.*

No statute of limitations shall be made for the crimes of sexual abuse of a person younger than 18 years of age, or for rape, incest, or premeditated murder at any age.

No person shall be subject for the same offense to be put in jeopardy of life or limb *except in cases of jury tampering, destruction of evidence, bribery, or compelling new evidence of unjust conviction.*

No person shall be compelled in any criminal case to be a witness against himself, nor be deprived of life, liberty, or property without due process of law. *No accused person or any witness shall be subjected to any physical, mental, or emotional abuse while in the presence or custody of law enforcement.*

No person shall suffer the loss of private property taken for public *or private use* without just compensation *approved by a court of law.*

Discussion of Justification for the Changes

The people most likely adversely impacted by the crime are likely to live in proximity to where it occurred and have the strongest claim to be able to witness the trial. Repeated delays in incarceration of the guilty, increased costs to the public, and unnecessary crowding of court calendars occur when there is a prolonged dripping of appeals. However, justice requires a new trial or dismissal of charges when new evidence is discovered that suggests that the person may, in fact, be innocent.

Jury tampering, destruction of evidence, and bribery are not only additional new crimes, they may have resulted in a false verdict of innocence. Such a verdict should not be allowed to stand when it occurred because of a deliberate crime. The accused should be tried again with a new jury and a trial that allows introduction of the evidence of the original crime and of the new allegations of the additional crimes added to the indictment. To call such an outcome double jeopardy is to distort the meaning of a fair and impartial trial.

Section 2: Criminal Prosecutions

In all criminal prosecutions, the accused shall have the right to a speedy and public trial. *"Speedy" shall mean within 6 months of arrest, if incarcerated while awaiting trial. "Public" shall mean victims, the press, and media shall be allowed to record testimony and questioning in order to promote honesty and fairness in its representation to the public. Any person found innocent at trial shall be entitled to compensation for time imprisoned in a federal facility at a rate to be determined by Congress.*

The jury shall be in the State and district wherein the crime was committed, *and impartial in the opinion of the presiding judge(s). Change of venue shall be allowed only when compelling evidence is presented that the accused will not be able to receive a fair trial in the present location. Any and all appeals after conviction shall all be presented at the same time and to the appeals court responsible for the area where the crime occurred, except that a new appeal shall be permitted at any time when compelling evidence of innocence is discovered at a later time.*

Discussion of Justification for the Changes

A potentially innocent person being forced to wait more than 6 months without trial seems unreasonable, and innocent people should be compensated for their lost income.

(Continued revised text)

The accused shall be informed of the nature and cause of the accusation *at the time of arrest or arraignment in Court, the right to counsel, and that anything said or done while in the presence of law enforcement can be used against the accused in a court of law.* The accused shall have the right to be confronted by witnesses in person *for and against the accused, or virtually when the accused has a history of violence or anger mismanagement.*

The accused shall have the assistance of counsel for defense provided by the Court if able to prove that adequate counsel is beyond the financial ability of the accused.

Discussion of Justification for the Changes

The Miranda rights are an example of law made by court precedent. Including the wording here makes it law by Constitutional inclusion, removing any possible taint of unconstitutional lawmaking by the courts.

Section 3: Common Law Cases

In suits at common law, where the value in the controversy shall exceed *one hundred dollars,* the right of trial by jury shall be preserved, and no proven or stipulated fact tried by the jury shall be otherwise re-examined in any court of the United States, than according to the rules of the common law.

The enumeration in this Constitution of certain rights shall not be construed to deny or disparage others retained by the people.

Discussion of Justification for the Changes

The raising of the monetary limit for this provision is to allow somewhat for inflation since 1787.

Section 4: Bail

Excessive bail shall not be required, nor excessive fines imposed, nor cruel and unusual punishments inflicted.

Section 5: Extent of Judicial Power

The judicial power of the United States shall not be construed to extend to any suit in law or equity, commenced or prosecuted against one of the United States by citizens of another State, or by citizens or subjects of a foreign state.

Section 6: Limits of this Constitution

The powers not delegated to the United States by this Constitution, nor prohibited by it to the States, are reserved to the States respectively, or to the People.

★ ★ ★

Article IX:
Other Amendments and Changes
in the Constitution of 1787

Section 1: Abolishing the Electoral College

Adoption of this Constitution shall immediately abolish the Electoral College. The election of the President and Vice-President of the United States and all federal elective offices shall be determined by who wins the greatest number of the votes cast by the citizens of the United States and its Territories during federal elections.

Section 2: Slavery Is Forbidden

Neither slavery nor involuntary servitude, except as a lawful punishment for crime of the party duly convicted, shall exist within any place subject to the jurisdiction of the United States.

Congress shall have the power to enforce this article by appropriate legislation.

Section 3: Citizenship by Birth and Citizen Rights

All persons born *legally* or naturalized in the United States, including Native Americans, and subject to the jurisdiction thereof, are citizens of the United States *and of the State wherein they reside at the time of birth or naturalization, unless neither parent is a U.S. citizen but shall automatically become a citizen after residing in the United States or one of its Territories or Possessions for 12 continuous calendar months after birth. Proof of meeting these requirements shall be presented to a federal immigration office before documentation of citizenship is provided.*

No State shall make or enforce any law which shall abridge the privileges or immunities of citizens of the United States, nor shall any State deprive any person of life, liberty, or property, without the due process of law, nor deny to any person within its jurisdiction the equal protection of the laws, *nor the right to vote if that person is a citizen who has reached the proper age and is not imprisoned for rebellion or a felony. Children born to an America citizen living outside the territory subject to the United States of America shall be granted citizenship if that person meets the qualifications specified in United States law.*

Discussion of Justification for the Changes

These changes enshrine current law into a Constitutional provision for children of a citizen born outside the United States of America.

This provision also denies citizenship to babies born here as part of the practice of entering the United States just to deliver a baby, so that it will have citizen status and benefits whenever it crosses back into the United States, unless it maintained residency for 12 continuous months after birth.

Section 4: Dual Citizenship Not Allowed;
Representation in Congress

Representatives *and Senators* shall be apportioned among the several States according to their respective numbers, counting the whole number of persons in each state.

Undivided citizen loyalty precludes dual citizenship, so no United States Citizen shall have dual citizenship after this Constitution is adopted. All those who currently hold such dual citizenship must renounce all except their American citizenship and submit a notarized letter to the nearest federal office of immigration in the United States of America within six months that they have done so or forfeit their American citizenship.

Discussion of Justification for the Changes

Although some Native Americans are not taxed, Congress, from time to time, does make laws that impact these same persons, so they should be granted representation by being allowed to vote in federal elections.

In the past, American citizens have been allowed to maintain dual citizenship—a practice that divides their loyalty and should not be allowed. No person can serve two masters; eventually the needs of one will require disloyalty to the other.

Section 5: Right to Vote Begins at Age 18 Years

But when the right to vote at any federal election or for the Executive and Judicial officers of a State or members of the legislature thereof, is denied to any of the citizens of such State being *eighteen years* of age *or older* and who are of the United States *or its Territories,* or in any way abridged, except for participation in rebellion, *insurrection,* or other crime, the basis of representation therein shall be reduced in the proportion which the number of such citizens shall bear to the whole number of citizens *eighteen years* of age *or older* in such State.

Discussion of Justification for the Changes

The legal age for voting in federal elections was changed, but this provision was not updated within the written Constitution; now it is.

Section 6: Not Serve in Any Public Office if Part of an Insurrection or Rebellion

No person shall be a Senator or Representative in Congress, or hold any office, civilian or military, under the United States, or under any State, who, having previously taken an oath, as a member of Congress, or as any officer of the United States, or as a member of any State legislature, or as an executive or judicial officer of any State *at any time and for any reason taken an oath to support and defend* the Constitution of the United States shall have engaged in insurrection or rebellion against the same, or given aid or comfort to the enemies thereof.

Peaceful protest of a grievance being excepted.

Discussion of Justification for the Changes

All circumstances for taking the oath should now be covered for the future.

Peaceful protest is allowed under this Constitution and should not be forbidden here.

Section 7: The National Debt

The validity of public debt of the United States, authorized by law, including debts incurred for payment of pensions and bounties for service in suppressing insurrection or rebellion, shall not be questioned. *The national debt ceiling shall be raised whenever necessary to pay such debt and ensure the safety and security of any debt obligations incurred in a lawful manner by the United States.*

Discussion of Justification for the Changes

The faith, credit, and economic supremacy of the United States and the economic security of the world, to a great extent, depend on the world's faith in our honoring our economic, political, and treaty obligations. We must never create circumstances where these are called into question if we wish to remain economically and politically trusted.

Section 8: Illegal Debt

But neither the United States nor any State shall assume or pay any debt or obligation incurred in aid of insurrection or rebellion against the United States, or any claims for loss; but all such debts, obligations, and claims shall be held illegal and void.

Section 9: Enforcement

The Congress shall have the power to enforce, by appropriate legislation, the provisions of this article.

ARTICLE X

Section 1: Right to Vote

The right of citizens of the United States *and its Territories* to vote shall not be denied or abridged by the United States or by any State or Territory on account of race, color, *religion, sexual orientation, or previous condition of servitude or imprisonment if all terms, paroles, fines, restitutions, and punitive conditions have been completed.*

The Congress shall have the power to enforce this article by appropriate legislation.

Section 2: Closing Taxation Loopholes

The Congress shall have the power to lay and collect taxes on incomes, from whatever source derived, without apportionment among the States, and without regard to any census or enumeration, *including but not limited to the value of stock options at the value when purchased minus actual price paid, with the difference being taxed as received income in the tax year of the purchase, money borrowed from any asset, including but not limited to trusts, 401k, retirement-deferred income, annuity, education funds, and money borrowed on real estate not used for repairs or improvement to the property, shall be taxable as income in the year borrowed, even if the interest is not tax-deductible.*

Discussion of Justification for the Changes

In recent years, the wealthy have been borrowing from tax shelters so as to be able to use money without paying taxes. This loophole is not likely to be closed by politicians, since it benefits their donors. By putting this into this Constitution, the average citizen is given the opportunity to decide on its merits.

Section 3: Repeal of the 17th Amendment of the 1787 Constitution

Article X, Subsection 1, hereby repeals the 17th Amendment, since this Constitution changes the number of Senators for each State based on population and abolishes the Electoral College.

Section 4: Repeal of the 18th Amendment of the 1787 Constitution

Article X, Subsection 2 hereby declares that the former 18th Amendment was repealed by the 21st Amendment, and, therefore, both are no longer needed, and the use of intoxicating beverages is now a subject for the individual States to decide.

Section 5: Vote and Identity

Article X, Subsection 3 hereby reaffirms that the right to vote and all other rights of American citizens shall not be denied or abridged by the United States or by any State on account of sexual identity.

Congress shall have the power to enforce Article X and the Subsections therein by appropriate legislation.

ARTICLE XI

(Amendments to the 1787 Constitution)

Section 1) Beginning of Terms of Office

The terms of the President and Vice-President shall end at noon on the 20th day of January, and the terms of Senators and Representatives at noon on the 3rd day of January, of the years *specified in this Constitution, and the terms of their successors shall then begin.*

Section 2) Start of Congressional Sessions

The Congress shall assemble at least once in every year, and such meeting shall begin at noon on the 3rd day of January, unless they shall by law appoint a different day.

Section 3) Succession in Executive Branch if President-Elect Dies

If, at the time fixed for the beginning of the term of President, the President-Elect shall have died, the Vice-President-Elect shall become the President. If a President shall not have been chosen before the time fixed for the beginning of the term, or if the President-Elect shall have failed to qualify, then *the President in office shall continue to be temporary President and shall by Executive Order have a new election held 30 days after the vacancy occurred and the President and Vice-President shall temporarily continue the duties of those offices for 90 days and extended an additional thirty days until both the offices are filled in a new election. If no qualified candidate is elected to each office, a second national election shall be held in 30 calendar days, and if no qualified candidate is elected to each office, this process shall be repeated every 30 calendar days until qualified persons are elected to both offices.*

Section 4) Death of the Speaker of the House or President of the Senate (Vice-President)

The Congress may by law provide for the case of the death of any of the persons from whom the House of Representatives may choose a Speaker whenever the right choice shall have devolved upon them, but for the case of the *vacancy of the President of the Senate, the major-ity leader of the Senate shall assume the duties and responsibilities of the*

Vice-President until a new Vice-President is elected. A national election shall be declared by the President, by Executive Order, for that purpose including only candidate from the same politicalm party as the President and occur within 90 ndays of the vacancy of the office of Vice-President and once every 30 days thereafter until a qualified new Vice-President is elected.

Discussion of Justification for the Changes

The President and Vice-President should always be chosen by a vote of the people. In a democracy, we should never have executives who were not chosen by the people.

Section 5: 21st Amendment to the 1787 Constitution

The 18th Article of Amendment to the Constitution of 1787 of the United States is hereby repealed.

Section 6: Limitation of the Presidency to two terms (22nd Amendment to the 1787 Constitution)

No person shall be elected to the office of President more than twice, and no person who has held the office of President, or acted as President for more than two years of a term to which some other person was elected President, shall be elected to the Office of President more than once. But this article shall not apply to any person holding the office of President when this Article was proposed to Congress, and shall not prevent any person who may be holding the office of President, or acting as President, during the term within which this Article becomes operative, from holding the office of President or acting as President during the remainder of such term.

This provision is added to this Constitution by this Section.

Section 7: Repeal of the 23rd Amendment to the 1787 Constitution.
The 23rd Amendment to the Constitution is hereby repealed, since the Electoral College is abolished by Article IX, Subsection 1a, of this Constitution.

Section 8; Taxes and Voting Rights (the 24th Amendment to the 1787 Constitution)
The rights of citizens of the United States to vote in any primary or other election for President or Vice-President, or for Senator or Representative in Congress, shall not be denied or abridged by the United States or by any State by reason of failure to pay poll tax *or other taxes related to voting rights imposed by any State.*

The Congress shall have the Power to enforce *or change* this article by appropriate legislation.

Discussion of Justification for the Changes

This Constitution abolishes the Electoral College.

Section 9: Replacement of President or Vice-President When There Is a Vacancy. (25th Amendment to the 1787 Constitution)

Sections 1 and 2 of the 25th Amendment to the 1787 Constitution are hereby repealed and replaced by Article XI, Sections 3 and 4.

ARTICLE XII

(Formerly Sections 3 and 4 of the 25th Amendment to the 1787 Constitution)

Section 1

Whenever the President transmits to the President pro tempore of the Senate and the Speaker of the House of Representatives his written declaration that he is unable to discharge the powers and duties of his office, and until he transmits to them in a written declaration to the contrary, such powers and duties shall be discharged by the Vice-President as Acting President.

Section 2

If within 120 days of the initial letter of disability the President transmits to the President pro tempore of the Senate and the Speaker of the House of Representatives the President's written declaration that no inability exists, the President shall resume the powers and duties of the office of President unless the Vice-President and a majority of the principal officers of the Executive Branch or such other body as Congress may, by law, provide, transmit within four days to the President pro tempore of the Senate and the Speaker of the House of Representatives their written declaration that the President is still unable to discharge the powers and duties of the office. Thereupon, Congress shall decide the issue, assembling in person or virtually, with adequate safety precautions, within 48 hours for that purpose in Special Session. If the Congress determines by a two-thirds vote of both Houses that the President is unable to discharge the powers and duties of the office of President, the Vice-President shall resume the powers and duties of the Presidency and begin the procedures specified in Article XI.

ARTICLE XIII

No law varying the compensation for the services of Senators and Representatives shall take effect until an election of Representatives shall have intervened.

★ ★ ★

CHAPTER 19

The Constitution for the 21st Century

Preamble

We, the People of the United States of America, now live in a different world than when our original Constitution was written in 1787 and adopted in 1788. Many unforeseen events, customs, ethical variations, political institutions, social, economic, technological, and population changes have transpired in the interim. Therefore, it is necessary to bring the Constitution of the United States into the 21st century, with modernizing revisions to better define and protect the rights and responsibilities of all citizens, in order to form an even more perfect Democracy, provide for the common domestic and foreign defense, promote the general Health, Welfare, Rights, and Safety, and to secure the maximum Blessings of Liberty. In the interest of Equality and Justice to ourselves and future posterity, we ordain and adopt this more modern Constitution of the United States of America.

ARTICLE I

Section 1: The Legislative Branch

All legislative Powers herein granted shall be vested in a Congress of the United States, which shall consist of a Senate and House of Representatives. No laws shall be made by the Executive or Judicial Branches by decree or judicial decision, except when granted by a law of Congress which specifies the duration and limits of the temporary authority established by both Houses of Congress. These Executive Orders or Temporary Court Decisions allowed may be made permanent by Congress as a new law before the temporary authority period ends, otherwise, all laws and executive orders issued under this temporary authority become inactive and unenforceable after the Sunset Date set when the temporary authority was established. The Judicial Branch shall not decide the intent of a law, since it did not make the law. Only Congress can specify the intent, and, if this is not clear, the Judicial Branch should send the law back to the Legislative Branch for clarification of the intent within the law.

Section 2: The House of Representatives

Subsection 2a) Term of Office
The House of Representatives shall be composed of Members chosen every four years by a majority of citizens with the right to vote in a Congressional Representation District. The Congressional Representation Districts shall be established by the National Federal Redistricting Board established by Section 3 of this Article and established as equally as possible, based on population data of the most recent national census, within each of the several States for each election.

The names and total votes for every candidate for federal office from all Federal Congressional Representation Districts shall be sent to the Executive of the State, in which case they are to be certified and forwarded to the National Redistricting Board headquarters in the federal capital for counting in the presence of at least one Representative of the House, Senate, Executive, and Judiciary Branches and determining the winners of seats in each district. The Board will then notify the candidates, the President, the Speaker of the House, the President of the Senate, and appropriate media, of the results.

Subsection 2b) Procedure for Beginning New Four-Year Terms

Immediately after they shall be assembled in consequence of the first election, all Members elected to the House of Representatives shall be divided as equally as may be into two classes by the Federal National Redistricting Board, with the number of members of a political party in each class as equal as possible. The Representatives of the first class who were reelected shall begin their term of office, as usual, at the end of the recent two-year term and serve for two more years. New members in this class will serve only two years before their seat is again up for election. Those of the second class shall begin on the same date but continue for the new term length of four years.

Thereafter, all terms shall have a length of four years unless terminated by impeachment, recall by the voters, resignation, illness or death, or on account of malfeasance, dereliction of duties, violation of oath of office, or conviction for a felony that would impede the ability of the member to perform the duties of their office. If vacancies happen before the next scheduled election for that position, and more than 120 days remain in that term, the Executive of the State shall appoint a Temporary Interim Representative from the same political party as the vacated Member to fill the position until the next regularly scheduled election for the House for that position.

Subsection 2c) Size of the House of Representatives

The total number of Member Representatives in the House shall not exceed 450. Each Representative shall represent an approximately equal number of people as closely as possible while not exceeding a total limit of 450 Members in the House of Representatives.

Subsection 2d): Qualifications for Representatives

No person shall be a Representative who shall not have attained the age of eighteen years and been six years a citizen of the United States. A person may seek elective office to the House of Representatives only if that person has resided in a congressional district in which that person has legally maintained primary residence for a minimum of 365 days before the election and continues to maintain primary residence for the entire term of representation. "Primary residence" shall mean occupation for 365 days each calendar year, except that days serving in the national capital can also count as days at the in-state primary residence. If a member moves out of the district represented, that member must immediately resign.

Subsection 2e) Filling Vacancies in the House of Representatives

When vacancies open in the federal Congressional representation from any State, the governor of that State shall order an election in the district represented by the vacancy, to be held within 60 calendar days of the beginning of the vacancy unless fewer than 120 calendar days remain in the term of the vacancy. All candidates seeking to be elected to fill out the remainder of the vacant term must meet age and citizenship requirements, be free of any impediments established by federal law, and register with the State office in charge of elections at least 30 days before the election.

Subsection 2f) Choosing Speaker of the House of Representatives and Rules for Each Session of Congress

The House of Representatives shall choose their Speaker upon the opening of each new Congress, after all new Members have been sworn in by the outgoing Speaker or new majority leader in the absence of the outgoing Speaker.

The Congress shall assemble at least every calendar year for a total of not less than 200 calendar days, except on Saturdays and Sundays, unless they choose to meet more often. The House of Representatives and the Senate may choose to allow virtual attendance and voting at committee and general sessions, with necessary security provisions. The presence of a quorum of the House Membership shall be required to conduct any business, to debate, or to give speeches. Closed-door sessions shall be limited to items of national security and in-person attendance only.

Section 3: Federal Congressional Redistricting Board: Qualifications, Duties, and Procedure for Appointing Federal Congressional Redistricting Board Members and Their Compensation

Subsection 3a) Qualifications, Procedures, Terms of Office of Federal Congressional Redistricting Board Members

Determination of District boundaries for Federal Congressional Representatives shall be determined by a Federal Congressional Redistricting Board, consisting of two resident citizens from each State, nominated by the President and approved by a simple majority vote in both Houses of Congress, none of whom shall have held public office, been an officer of any political party, been convicted of any felony, been a political lobbyist, or engaged in any illegal activity with regard to any form of public service. Redistricting shall be completed within six months of completion of each official ten-year National Census and whenever circumstances so require. The first group shall be appointed in the first twelve months following adoption of this Constitution and serve a minimum term of 10 years or longer but ending on the first day of January of the next year ending in "5" after serving at least 10 years. Each Board member appointed thereafter shall serve for ten years starting on the 1st of January in years ending in "5."

The goal of the Federal Congressional Redistricting Board within each state shall be to have the total of such districts within a State reflect the political, ethnic, and cultural composition of that State as closely as possible so that Members-elect sent to the House of Representatives and Senate will, as closely as possible, be based on the most recent census data. All voters in a Federal Congressional District must be in the same contiguous geographic area.

Subsection 3b)

Congress shall determine the annual compensation and travel and lodging allotments for Members to attend Federal Congressional Redistricting Board meetings in the national capital. The members shall not accept any other form of compensation or emolument for activities related to their duties as Board members, as that might give the appearance of attempting to influenece any member's decisions.

Subsection 3c)

The Congress shall have the Power to enforce this Section by appropriate legislation or by Constitutional Amendment.

Section 4: Procedure for Voters to Recall a Member of the House of Representatives or Senate.

If 10 percent of the registered voters of a Congressional District sign a Petition for Recall for their elected Congressional Member and present this petition to the Office of the Governor of that State or equivalent territorial executive, that official shall call for a Special Recall Referendum and Replacement Vote to be held throughout that District or Territorial region represented by the Member within

60 calendar days of the date the Petition was presented if more than 120 calendar days remain in the term of that Member. Congressional candidates may participate as possible replacements as Representatives or Senators from that District by filing applications. All candidates seeking to be elected to fill out the remainder of the vacant term must meet age and citizenship requirements, be free of any impediments established by federal law, and register with the government office in charge of elections for that Congressional position at least 30 days before the recall/replacement election. Voters will then vote on a ballot containing a Yes/No vote on the Recall and a first and second choice for a replacement. If the final vote is a majority of Yes votes for Recall, the new candidate with the most combined first- and second-choice votes will be elected to fill the remainder of the vacated position in the House of Representatives or Senate. If fewer than 120 days remain in the term, the seat shall remain vacant until the next regularly scheduled election for that seat in the House of Representatives.

Section 5: Federal Impeachment

Subsection 5a) Power to Impeach

Power of Impeachment of any federal office holder in Congress, the Executive, or Judicial Branch, regardless of how that person was elected, appointed, or otherwise came to occupy their position of public service, shall be possible by the House of Representatives or Senate.

Subsection 5b) Impeachment Trials

Judgement in Cases of Impeachment of any Federal Official elected or hired shall, henceforth, be by a jury of twelve citizens selected in the manner of all other criminal proceedings, since all citizens must be treated as Equals before the Law, and the proceedings should not be influenced by political bias. If the official is found guilty, punishment shall be according to Law for the offense, except in cases of treason or espionage, when the punishment shall be life in prison without pardon or parole. Treason shall constitute giving aid or comfort to an enemy of the United States that threatens the national security in time of peace or war, except as part of negotiations for a treaty of peace, or end of hostilities.

Subsection 5c) Grounds for Impeachment
Charges for Impeachment shall include but not be limited to:

1. Repeated false or deliberate misleading campaign statements;

2. Misuse of campaign funds for personal or non-campaign use;

3. Withholding the truth, or providing false or misleading information during appointment or other Congressional testimony except for withholding information related to national security during a public hearing or when such testimony may be covered by protections from self-incrimination or valid attorney-client privilege.

4. Conviction of a capital crime;

5. Participation in expressed or material support for insurrection or violence against a duly elected government administration or individual;

6. Failure to uphold the oath to defend the Constitution of the United States;

7. Failure by a public official or military personnel, including civilians in government service, to report to proper authority suspicion of or witnessing improper possession and/or

distribution of materials that might jeopardize the security of the United States when other civilian or military justice systems fail to do so;

8. Any additional reason the House or Senate shall deem appropriate and make law.

Subsection 5d) Procedure for Impeachment Investigation

The House of Representatives or Senate shall within four weeks from the date of choosing to investigate accusations for possible Impeachment, select a Special Temporary Impeachment Investigation Committee of nine of its members, four from each of the two major political parties recognized on the federal ballot and one person of another or no party affiliation chosen jointly by the leaders of the remaining minor parties on the federal ballot if no person of another or no party affiliation was elected to the House or Senate Chamber seeking Impeachment. When all Members of the Congressional Chamber involved belong to one or the other of only two parties, the ninth member shall be chosen by the Party by a two-sided coin toss. The losing party in the toss would pick a member of the winning party to fill the ninth position.

The Special Temporary Impeachment Investigation Committee shall be limited to investigating information related to the charges for possible Impeachment.

Subsection 5e) Powers and Terms of a Special Temporary Impeachment Investigation Committee

The Special Temporary Impeachment Investigation Committee shall have power to subpoena all people serving in any federal elected or administrative office, including President, Vice-President, Cabinet Secretary or subordinate, Member of Congress, or member of the Federal Judiciary, including the Supreme Court, Federal Reserve Board, or National Redistricting Board, or any citizen believed to have significant information. Charges for impeachment investigation shall be initiated by a majority vote in the House or Senate.

1. The subpoena power of this committee shall be enforceable for every person in the jurisdiction of the United States of America, regardless of any political office or status.

2. The Special Temporary Impeachment Investgation Committee shall have a six-month term to complete its investigation from the date of acceptance of its ninth member and submit a recommendation in writing to the full House or Senate, as appropriate, at the end of the investigation. Only the full House or Senate, by majority vote, shall have the power to issue Articles of Impeachment against any official of the United States government, including, but not limited to, the President, Vice-President, Secretaries of the Executive Branch, justices of the Judiciary Branch, including the Supreme Court and any other federal court, or Senators and Members of the House while in office or after leaving office for offenses while in office, since these trials will henceforth be comparable to all other jury trials.

3. The House of Representatives or Senate may extend the term of investigation with new limits for the Special Temporary Committee for Impeachment Investigation by majority vote of all the members when the evidence gathered appears to justify an extension. There shall be no statute of limitations for these provisions, because their possible impact may affect all people within the jurisdiction of the United States of America beyond the foreseeable future. The sole exceptions for terminating these proceedings shall be when there is sufficient evidence to proceed, the accused is found to be innocent by a jury, or the person has died.

Subsection 5f) Sanctions for Failure to Comply with a Subpoena Regarding Impeachment Shall Be Imprisonment

Failure to appear when subpoenaed by a Committee or Subcommittee of Congress of any person when related to Constitutional violations by a public servant without justifiable medical cause for not appearing shall result in imprisonment for up to 12 months, and removal from holding public office for up to one year including loss of wages and benefits while incarcerated. Imprisonment shall cease earlier if the person appears in response to the subpoena.

Such confinement shall begin one day after the date to appear and shall continue for up to one calendar year unless the subpoenaed individual submits to appear, and that person shall be released on the first day of testimony or at the end of one calendar year. Removal from office for failure to appear shall cease on the 365th day of imprisonment, or upon completion of testimony unless the person is a target of the investigation, or the charges are dismissed by the Committee or a vote of the full House or Senate involved.

1. Any federal-government official shall cease to exercise all duties of their position, if imprisoned or Impeached, until the end of their testimony for subpoenaed witnesses or in the case of an indictment or a vote to Impeach from the House of Representatives or Senate, the end of the Impeachment trial, if not found guilty, and for the duration of the sentence if found guilty while awaiting any appeal decisions.

2. If a Member of the Executive or Judicial Branch is found to be guilty in a court of law and imprisoned for any reason, that individual shall cease to exercise the duties of that office and not receive any compensation related to that office unless exonerated by a not-guilty verdict or hung jury. The person next in the Order of Succession shall assume the duties of the

incarcerated person until charges are dismissed or sentence is completed. If the imprisoned person is found guilty of a felony, they shall be permanently removed from office and shall be ineligible to hold any public office or employment for life.

3. If a Member of Congress or the Supreme Court is Impeached, that person shall immediately cease to exercise all duties of that office until found innocent or the charges are dropped by a 51 percent vote of the Chamber of Congress that initiated the Impeachment process.

Subsection 5g) Impeachment Trial Judges and Jury

Impeachment trials shall be presided over by three federal judges on the nearest Court of Appeals to the site of the alleged transgressions. The Jury shall consist of twelve citizens and four alternates who reside in the State or Territory in which the most serious charges occurred, none of whom shall be a current or past public official or political-party officer at any level or a lobbyist to any level of government officials or personnel. All jury members shall be chosen under the usual procedures and rules of federal court to preside and render a verdict and prescribe the punishment if none is otherwise provided or required by federal law.

Subsection 5h) Prosecutors and Defenders

Prosecution shall be by attorneys from the Justice Department. Defense shall be by the defendant's chosen team of attorneys licensed to practice law in the jurisdiction where the trial is held or by a public defender appointed by the three-judge panel presiding, when the defendant can be proven not to be able to afford legal counsel. Agreeing to be a public defender when necessary shall be a condition for being allowed to practice law in a federal court. If more than one attorney is chosen by the defendant, the defendant shall be responsible for all attorney's fees.

Subsection 5i) Compensation for Public Defender

Congress shall have the power to determine fair compensation for public defenders in such cases.

Subsection 5j) Public Contribution for Defense

Costs of Impeachment trial defense assistance shall not be made by any citizen contribution of a total of $100 or more in value to all funds or individuals in public or private. This maximum amount allowed shall change based on the national rate of inflation or deflation of the value of the national currency. A list of the names and contributions of any donations or gifts shall be submitted to the Attorney General on a monthly basis by the defendant or the defendant's attorney until all such activities have ceased, in order to prevent abuse or attempts to buy favors. Donors shall not use third parties to finance or tender additional donations.

Subsection 5k)

Congress shall have power to provide for this provision by appropriate legislation.

Section 6: The Senate

Subsection 6a) Number, Terms, and Districts

The Senate shall be composed of an equal number of Members as the House of Representatives but never exceeding 450. Terms will be for six years in the Senate. The Senate districts shall be divided into three groups of as equal size as is practicable, so that the population represented by each Senator is as fair as possible among all the States as it is in the House of Representatives. The Federal Congressional

Redistricting Board shall determine the Senate District Boundaries within six months after each census and whenever necessary for lawful reasons. If a State is scheduled to hold a new election because the State has lost position(s) before the terms of existing Senators has expired, the longest-serving members from that state must resign on the date set for swearing-in of the new members of the Senate.

Subsection 6b) Residence Requirement for Congressional Senators

No Person shall be a Senator who shall not have attained the age of 18 years and been 10 years a citizen of the United States. Persons may seek elective office to the Senate only if they have legally maintained continuous primary residence in that Senate district for a minimum of 10 years before the election and continue to maintain primary residence for the entire term in the Senate. "Primary residence" shall mean establishment and maintenance of a primary residence in that district for continuous 365 days. Days serving in the national capital can also count as days at the in-state primary residence.

Subsection 6c) Phase-In of New Senators

In the first Senate election immediately after the implementation of this new Constitution, all new Senate seats shall be divided into three groups of about equal size by the President of the Senate. All Senators who have not finished their full six-year term shall remain in office until their six-year term is completed and be assigned to the appropriate group depending on the number of remaining years in their term.

The first group of Senator seats to face a new election shall be for six-year terms and include those full terms just terminated.

The second group will be for two-year terms, so that the end of these terms coincide with those Senators who had two years remaining in their original terms when the change in number of seats was implemented. All of these seats will then come up for re-election at the next regular Senate election after that and be for six years.

The third group will be for four-year terms, so that the end of these terms coincides with those Senators who had four years remaining in their original terms when the change in number of seats was implemented. All of these seats will then come up for re-election at the next regular Senate election after that and be for six years.

Thereafter, all seats will be subject to election on a six-year cycle except for unexpected early vacancies.

Subsection 6d) Redistricting after Each Census

Within six months of each ten-year census, the National Federal Election Board shall determine the federal Senate Districts for each state, which may, but do not have to exactly, match those for the House of Representatives districts.

Subsection 6e) Filling of Vacancies

When vacancies open in the federal Senate representation from any State, the Governor of that State shall order an election in the District represented by the vacancy, to be held within 60 calendar days of the beginning of the vacancy, unless fewer than 120 calendar days remain in the term of the vacancy. All candidates seeking to be elected to fill out the remainder of the vacant term must meet age and citizenship requirements, be free of any impediments established by federal law, and register with the State office in charge of elections at least 30 days before the election.

When one or more Senate or House of Representatives seats is lost by a State because of the new census, the longest-serving Senators and Representatives from that State must resign on the day before the opening of Congress, when the new Senator taking the seat from another State will be sworn in.

Subsection 6f) Temporary Offices in the Senate during Emergencies

The Vice-President of the United States shall be President of the Senate, but shall have no vote, unless the vote be equal. In the event that the Vice-President has to assume the duties of the President for fewer than 90 calendar days, the Vice-President shall nominate a successor of the same political party for Temporary Vice-President with the consent of a simple majority of the Senators of the same party to fill the position until the President is able to reassume the full duties of the office of the President. When the elected President returns to fulfill the duties of the office of the President, the Vice-President will return to the regular duties of that office, and the Temporary Vice-President shall resign from that office.

If the Vice-President has to assume the office of President for more than 120 days, the President shall resign, and the Temporary Vice-President shall remain in that office in the Senate until a new Vice-President is elected.

The House of Representatives and Senate may choose to allow virtual attendance and voting at committee and general sessions, with adequate security provisions. Closed-door sessions shall be limited to items of national security, and in-person attendance shall be mandatory for all members of the subcommittee, committee, or House of Representatives or Senate involved.

Section 6g) Elections

The times, types of places, and general rules for holding federal elections for all federal offices shall be prescribed by the Federal Congressional Redistricting Board for all States or by Law. The date shall be the first Monday in November and shall be a National Holiday. The choosing of election rules for federal elections such as hours, absentee ballots, voter identification, etc., shall be established by Law by the House of Representatives, Senate, and President of the United States.

Registered voters shall have the option of Absentee-voting in all federal elections for at least two calendar weeks before Voting Day. Individual States may grant longer periods. All such votes received within 10 days after election day shall be counted.

Section 7: Powers and Duties of Congress

Subsection 7a) Attendance

Each House shall be the judge of the qualifications and fitness of its own Members to serve. A majority must be present physically or virtually to constitute a quorum to conduct business except that a small number may vote to adjourn, or a quorum may unanimously vote to compel all absent members to attend by a certain date unless absent because of illness.

Absence from a session of Congress for foreign travel at taxpayer expense must be by prior legislative authorization of the travel and expenses, except when a national emergency has been declared by the President and the trip is related to that emergency declaration.

No federal money, equipment, travel, or privileges—or their equivalent—shall be used for campaign or other political purposes.

Subsection 7b) Procedures for Debate

All Members of either House—if in the chamber or virtually—shall be allowed and limited up to five minutes of debate on an individual bill and/or amendments before any Member is allowed an additional five-minute period.

No Member shall be allowed to filibuster any proposed legislation since this is an infringement on the representatives of all the other citizens' right to have their delegates and bill proposals heard and be debated.

When proposed legislation is presented by a member of a committee or subcommittee, all members shall be given a copy of the bill or resolution and one calendar week to review the proposal. One week from the date presented, or less if the committee or subcommittee so chooses, the committee or subcommittee shall vote by roll call as to whether to debate the measure. Committees must debate any issue or proposal when a majority of those present vote to have such a debate scheduled. No chairman or member shall have the power to prevent or delay such a debate without majority vote Senate or House of Representatives' approval by recorded majority vote.

Any bill submitted to a committee or directly as a bill to the entire chamber which has at least 46 co-sponsors must be accepted for debate and vote in any committee with jurisdiction and by the entire House of Representatives or Senate during a mandated attendance ordered by the Speaker of the House of Representatives or President of the Senate. Neither the Speaker of the House nor the President of the Senate shall prevent debate of any issue in which 25% or more of those present vote to open the debate.

Otherwise, each House may determine, by majority vote, the rules of its proceedings for each session, sanctions for any of its Members for disorderly behavior while in session, and with the concurrence of two thirds of its Members, temporarily suspend or permanently expel a Member.

Each House shall keep a Journal of its actual Proceedings and only of speeches as actually delivered, when in session, and, at least once each calendar month, publish the same, excepting such Parts as may in their judgment require secrecy for national security reasons; and the Yeas and Nays, absent, or abstentions of each Member of either House on all votes shall be entered into the Journal.

Neither House, during the Session of Congress, shall, without the consent of the other, adjourn for more than three days, nor to any location than that in which the two Houses shall be sitting except in an emergency, wherein no other possibility exists.

Section 7c) Rights and Disabilities of Members

The Senators and Representatives shall receive a compensation for their services, to be ascertained by law and paid out of the Treasury of the United States. They shall, in all cases, except conviction for treason, Impeachment, Felony, or Breach of Peace or Oath of Office, or arrest for a felony, physical assault, or threat of assault with a weapon against any citizen, not be subject to interference from attendance at the session of their respective Houses, and going to and returning from the same, and for any speech or debate in either House. They shall not be compelled to answer to questions in any other place except in response to a lawfully obtained subpoena.

No Senator or Representative shall, during the time for which he/she was elected or appointed to any civil office under the authority of the United States, accept any emolument, current or in the future, from any private or public entity doing business with the Federal government or a State government or the military, or receive any emoluments, gifts, free travel, lodging, meals, employment, or consulting fee from any such entity, individual or group, or political candidate for a period of five years after leaving office except as specifically allowed by law. No person holding any office under the authority of the United States shall also be a Member of either House during his/her continuance in office except as provided herein.

Section 8: Legislative Process, Veto Power, and Override of Supreme Court Decisions

Subsection 8a) Debt and Revenue

The debt limit must always be raised when necessary to pay for expenses of laws already enacted. All bills for raising revenue shall originate in the House of Representatives for debt payment or operation of the United States government so that it may perform its duties and pay its obligations, but the Senate may propose or concur with

Amendments to the same as on other proposed legislation. All new legislation requiring spending shall contain the means of paying for the program or services without borrowing except in national emergencies, so such legislation shall always originate in the House of Representatives.

Subsection 8b) Veto Power

Every bill which shall have passed the House of Representatives and the Senate, shall, before it becomes a law, be presented to the President of the United States; if the President approves and signs it, it shall become law unless declared unconstitutional by the Supreme Court of the United States. But if the President shall return it to the House in which it originated unsigned, with enumeration of the Executive Branch objections and their reasons to veto, the objections and reasons shall be listed in the Journal of that House except in cases involving national-security concerns. The House may then choose to reconsider the bill, and, if after reconsideration, two thirds by Roll Call Vote of the House shall agree to override the Presidential veto, it shall be sent again to the Senate, by which it will likewise be reconsidered, and if two thirds of the Senate shall also agree to override the Presidential veto by Roll Call Vote, it shall become law; the names and votes of all Members of both Houses shall be published in their respective Journals for the benefit of all citizens.

If any Bill shall not be returned by the President within ten Days (Sundays excepted) after it is presented to him, the same shall become the law as if signed by the President, unless the Congress, by adjournment before the ten-day period has occurred, prevent its return, in which case, it shall not be a law.

Every order, resolution, or vote to which concurrence may be necessary (except on the question of adjournment) shall be presented to the President of the United States, and before the same shall take effect, shall be approved by the President, or being disapproved by the President, shall be passed by two thirds of the Senate and House of Representatives, according to the same rules and limitations as a bill.

Subsection 8c) Override of Court Decisions

All Supreme Court decisions shall be subject to override by the Congress, or the people, subject to the following procedures and limitations.

If a Federal Court or the Supreme Court rules that any federal law or regulation is unconstitutional, it must return the law or regulation to the Congress and, if appropriate, the Executive Branch where it originated, with enumeration of the judiciary objections and reasons. The House or Senate which originated the law involved and was the source of its intention, may then choose to reconsider the law, and, after its reconsideration two thirds by Roll Call Vote of the one House shall agree to override the Federal or Supreme Court ruling of unconstitutionality, it shall be sent to the other House, by which it will likewise be reconsidered, and, if two thirds of that House shall also agree to override the Federal or Supreme Court ruling, by Roll Call Vote, it shall become a proposed Amendment to the Constitution and sent to the States for their vote as specified in Article V.

The names and votes of all Members of both Houses and the Supreme Court members shall be published in their respective Congressional Journals for the benefit of all citizens except in those cases involving national security.

If one per cent of eligible voters sign, and submit to the President of the Senate, a petition requesting that a Proposition be placed on the ballot of the next federal election, proposing an Amendment to this Constitution, the Proposition shall be placed as soon as possible on the next federal ballot. If a simple majority of voters approve the Proposition, it shall become a Constitutional Amendment effective at 00:01 on the first day of January of the next year.

Section 9: Powers of Congress

Only the National Federal Redistricting Board, with the consent of both houses of Congress, shall make the rules for election to federal offices, as specified herein, including the date, hours, types of places, and eligibility to vote. Congress may choose to delegate such duties to impartial, neutral parties at its discretion.

The Congress shall have power to lay and collect taxes, duties, imports and excises, to pay the debts and provide for the common defense and the general welfare of the United States and its citizens and occupants, but all federal taxes, duties, imports, and excises shall be uniform throughout the United States;

To borrow money and pay interest on the credit of the United States; this power shall be mandatory when raising the national debt to pay for money already borrowed.

To regulate commerce with foreign nations, and among the States, and the Territories, and with the Native American Tribes;

To establish uniform rules of immigration and naturalization for new citizens, temporary visas for travel, education, or employment, and uniform laws on the subject of bankruptcies throughout the United States;

To coin and print money or the electronic equivalent, regulate the value thereof, and of foreign money within the United States and its jurisdiction, and fix the national standard of Weights and Measures;

To provide punishment of counterfeiting the securities and current money of the United States and of defrauding people in the United States by foreign or domestic individuals or other entities by scams, false advertising, computer malware, or hacking of electronic devices.

To establish Post Offices and special communication facilities in event of threatened hostilities, domestic or foreign;

To promote progress of science and the arts, by securing for limited times to authors and inventors, individuals and corporations, the exclusive right to their respective new writings, intellectual and structural creations, and discoveries.

To constitute federal tribunals inferior to the Supreme Court in any location deemed necessary for protecting equal justice and a fair and timely administration of the law;

To define and punish piracies and felonies committed against American citizens, property, or commercial or military interests on Earth, in Space or on any celestial body, and offenses against the law of nations;

To declare war, grant letters of marque and reprisal, and make rules concerning captures;

To exclusively raise and support all armed forces, including all militias except for State National Guards, local police, sheriffs, and marshals, and make appropriations of money to be used for those purposes specified in legislation for a specified period of time;

To make rules for the government and regulation of all federal forces bearing or not bearing arms for enforcement of federal laws or regulations;

To provide and call forth federally or other government-sanctioned militias to execute the laws of the United States, suppress domestic insurrections, and repel invasions when the governors of the States are unable or fail to do so in a timely manner, when more than one State is involved, or when a State requests aid from the President of the United States or the Vice-President if the President fails to respond, or Speaker of the House when the Executive Branch fails to respond in a timely manner.

To provide for organizing, arming, and disciplining militias and paying and governing them when employed in the service of the federal government, reserving to the States respectfully the appointment of officers, the training of the members according to the discipline and level of ability prescribed by Congress.

To exercise exclusive legislation in all cases, exclusive of appropriate authority for management of city government, over the District of

Columbia and all places purchased with the consent of the legislature of the State or Territory in which the same shall be located, for the establishment of military facilities, embassies, consulates, and other needful structures for the national security, and

To make all laws which shall be necessary and proper for carrying into execution the foregoing powers, and all other powers vested in this Constitution in the Government of the United States, or in any Department or Office thereof.

Section 10: Powers Denied Congress

The privilege of the Writ of Habeas Corpus shall not be suspended, unless, when in cases of rebellion or invasion, the public safety may require it.

No Bill of Attainder or *ex post facto* law shall be passed.

No Capitation, or other direct, tax shall be laid, unless in proportion to the census or enumeration herein before directed be taken.

No tax or duty shall be laid on articles or services exported from any State.

No preference shall be given by any regulation of commerce or revenue to the ports of one State over those of another, nor shall vessels bound to or from, one State, be obliged to end, clear, or pay duties in another.

No money shall be drawn from the Treasury, but in consequences of appropriations made by law, and a regular Statement of all public Money shall be published on at least a yearly basis.

No title of nobility shall be granted by the United States: And no person holding any office of profit or trust under them in Congress, shall, without the consent of the Congress, accept any present, emolument, office, promise of future employment, award or reward, or title, of any kind whatever, from any king, prince, or foreign State, individual, organization, business, or corporation that engages in business with a government entity for profit, while in office or for five years after leaving office.

Neither the House of Representatives nor the Senate shall give to its Members any financial or equivalent, insurance, or retirement benefits not already available to the average employed citizen except as specified herein.

After adoption of this Constitution, Members of both the House of Representatives and the Senate and their employees shall be allowed to participate in the Social Security Program and all other unemployment and retirement programs mandated or allowed by Congress for employed citizens of the United States, and no person shall be allowed to participate in any other financial, investment, or insurance programs limited only to federal employees.

New Members of Congress retiring or not re-elected will no longer be vested for full retirement benefits for less than 20 years of service, after adoption of this Constitution.

Section 11: Powers Denied to the States

No State shall enter into any treaty, alliance, or confederation; grant letters of marque and reprisal; coin or print money; emit bills of credit; make any thing but gold and silver coin or lawful money of the United States as tender in payment of debts; pass any bill of attainder, *ex post facto* law, or law impairing the Obligation of contracts, or grant any title of nobility or special privilege.

No State shall, without the consent of the Congress, lay any imposts or duties on imports or exports, except what may be absolutely necessary for executing its inspection laws; and the net produce of all duties and imposts, laid by any State on imports and exports, shall be for the use of the Treasury of the United States; and all such laws shall be subject to the revision and control of the Congress.

No State shall, without the consent of Congress, lay any duty of tonnage, keep troops, or ships, or other weapons or equipment of war or militias in times of peace without the specific consent of Congress, enter into any agreement or compact with another State, or with a foreign power, or engage in war, unless actually invaded, or in such imminent danger as not to admit for delay.

ARTICLE II

Section 1: The President

The Executive Power shall be vested in a President of the United States.

He shall hold his office during the term of four years, together with the Vice-President of the same political party, chosen for the same term, and both be elected as follows:

The United States, striving to be a Democracy of, by, and for the People, the direct vote of the People in each State and Territory of the United States of America who have reached the age of eighteen years on or before election day of that year shall be counted for federal offices without interference by any individual, organization, or agency. The governor or chief executive of that State or Territory shall make a list of all persons voted for, and the number of votes for each; which list they shall sign, certify, and seal in the presence of Members of the ruling bodies of that State or Territory, and transmit to the seat of government of the United States, directed to the President of the Senate. In the event that the governor of a State, or chief executive of a Territory, or the President of the Senate is incapacitated, the person who is next in the line of succession for that office, and available, shall assume those duties and, in signing the list, shall note why they were made responsible for signing or supervising the counting of the votes.

The President of the Senate, or required substitute, shall, in the presence of Members of the Senate and House of Representatives, open all the legitimate certificates, and the votes shall be counted. The person having the greatest number of votes of the citizens shall be the President-elect, to take the Oath of Office at noon on the next Inauguration Day. The person running with the President-elect for the office of Vice-President shall be the Vice-President-elect.

No person except a natural-born citizen of the United States, who has attained to the age of thirty-five years and has been a continuous resident within the United States or one of its Territories, except those who have been otherwise assigned or ordered by an agency or official of the United States government, for official duties, such as ambassadors, embassy employees, et al., to temporarily serve outside the United States, shall be eligible for the Office of President or Vice-President.

No federal official, including the President and Vice-President, shall be immune from indictment, trial while in office, or serving any sentence imposed by criminal or impeachment trial after removal from office, because of their conviction, since a Constitutional provision now exists for their replacement.

In case of the removal of the President from office, due to death, or imprisonment or a guilty verdict after impeachment or a Federal or State felony trial, resignation, inability to discharge the powers and duties of said Office, the Office and duties of the President shall pass to the Vice-President to finish the term.

When the Vice-President is required to replace the President, or the Vice-President is no longer able to perform the duties of that office as determined by a vote in the Senate of members of the same political party, an emergency national election shall be held within 90 days to elect a new Vice-President from candidates of the same political party. The candidate receiving the most votes, even if not a majority, shall take the oath of office and assume the duties within one week after the election.

The President and Vice-President shall receive, at stated times, for the services of their respective offices, a compensation, which shall be neither increased nor diminished during the term for which either shall have been elected. Any emolument, gift, or service received by either person of more than $100 while in either office shall be the property of the People of the United States and remain with the government when that person leaves office. Failure to do so shall be an Impeachable offense.

Before the President, Vice-President, or any federal officer assumes the duties of their office, they shall take the following Oath of Office, whenever possible covered live by public media or before an assembly of the American People and other public officials,

"I (the name of the person), do solemnly swear (or affirm) that I will faithfully execute the Office of the President of the United States (or the Office they are about to assume), and will to the best of my ability, preserve, protect, and defend the Constitution of the United States with malice toward none and for the equal benefit of all."

Section 2: Powers of the President

The President shall be Commander-in-Chief of all the armed forces of the United States, and the militia of all the states, when called into the actual service of the United States; the President may require the opinion, in writing, of the principal officer in each of the Executive Departments, upon any subject relating to the duties of their respective offices.

The President shall have Power:

By and with the advice and consent of the Senate, to make treaties, with the Senate voting on the proposal within 3 months of its submission to the Senate by the President, and it shall be approved, provided two thirds of the Senators present concur when a quorum is present;

Nominate, and by and with the advice and consent of the Senate, shall appoint qualified ambassadors, other public ministers and consul, judges of the Supreme Court, federal judges, officers of federal departments and agencies, and all other officers of the United States whose appointments are not herein otherwise provided for and which shall be established by law, but Congress, may, by law, vest the appointment of such inferior officers, as they think proper, in the President alone or in the heads of departments. If a vacancy occurs in any of these positions, the President must nominate a replacement within a month, and the Senate must vote on the nominee within two months of the nomination, as long as the required vote occurs before the President has left office.

Nominations by the President authorized by this Constitution shall be debated within the Senate within 30 calendar days. No delays may be imposed by Congress or any government employee or elected official except the President when the President is acting within the authority of the office. If the debate or a vote does not occur within 30 calendar days of the nomination, except during a recess of the Senate when the counting shall be suspended until the Senate reconvenes, the nominees shall be considered as accepted by all and appointed to the offices specified.

After proper vetting for qualifications and ethical standards, such nominees shall require the approval of a majority of a quorum of Senators except as otherwise provided.

The President shall have the power to temporarily fill all vacancies that may open during the recess of the Senate, by granting commissions which shall expire when the Senators reconvene and after votes on the permanent replacements submitted by the President within one week of the commencement of that Senate session.

The President shall have the power to delegate duties to the Vice-President for specified durations during the term in office.

Section 3: Additional Duties of the President

The President shall:

At least once per year, give to Congress information regarding the State of the Union, and recommend to their consideration such measures and goals as the President shall judge necessary and expedient to advance the welfare, safety, and national security of the citizens of the United States;

May, on extraordinary occasions or national emergencies or disasters, request in writing the convening of one or both Houses of Congress for advice and making of Laws to alleviate or assist in restoring the welfare of the citizens impacted;

In cases of disagreement between the Houses with respect to the time of adjournment, the President may adjourn them to such time as may be proper;

Receive ambassadors and other public ministers;

Negotiate the release or exchange of Americans imprisoned in other countries;

Take care that all federal laws be faithfully and properly executed;

Commission all officers of the United States and its armed forces and militias; with the advice and consent of the Senate within 30 days of the Presidential approval except during Senate recess when the counting shall be considered suspended until the Senate reconvenes; the nominees shall be considered accepted by all as accepted to the office and rank specified.

May, on extraordinary occasions, national emergencies, or disasters, request in writing the convening of the Supreme Court for a special session in order to consider and rule on an issue requiring the immediate attention of that Court.

Section 4: Removal from Office

The President, Vice-President, and all civil officers of the United States, shall be removed from office on conviction by a jury of citizens of an Impeachable offense, treason or espionage during time of peace or hostilities, bribery, failure to report emoluments, high crimes or felonies, and be barred for life from any public office or position of public trust.

Section 5: Powers Not Given to the President

The President shall not have the power to pardon persons accused or convicted of any crime, since the proper venue for judicial decisions shall be in the powers of Article III.

The President shall not use the military, or militias within the borders of the United States, except when asked to do so by the Governor of a State or Territory or to stop violence or insurrection when a State Executive appears to be unwilling or unable to do so. Whenever possible, the President should do so with the advice and consent of the Senate, unless time is of the essence to save lives as determined by the Joint Chiefs of Staff.

ARTICLE III

Section 1: Structure of the Judicial Branch

Subsection 1a) Appointment, Term, and Age
The judicial power of the United States shall be vested in one Supreme Court, and in such lower courts as the Congress may from time to time establish by law.

All federal judges, including the Supreme Court, shall serve a term of ten years unless renominated by the President and reconfirmed by the

Senate. Terms shall last only until 70 years of age unless renominated and reconfirmed on a yearly basis thereafter. Any justices currently serving on a federal court bench who has or will attain the age of 69 must tender their resignation to the President on their 70th birthday. Each judge must then be renominated or replaced by the President with the concurrence of Congress by roll-call vote. Judges older than the age of 70 shall be subject to renomination on a yearly basis thereafter. More than one lower-court judge may be nominated and voted on simultaneously, unless 10 or more Senators object in writing to the President to one or more choices. These choices must then be withdrawn or considered individually by a quorum of the Senate.

The Supreme Court shall consist of nine judges nominated by the President and approved by a two-thirds majority of those present during a quorum of the Senate within 60 days of the nomination. One year after the adoption of this Constitution, any federal judge serving shall resign, including Supreme Court justices, if older than age 70. New judges may begin the new 10 year term as soon as the Senate approves the nominations. At least six months before each new term is to begin, the President shall submit, after proper vetting, the names of three nominees in the order of preference for each vacant Supreme Court position. If all three nominees are rejected, the President shall nominate three more until all vacant positions are filled and as needed thereafter.

Judges for lower courts may be selected in a group, which the Senate shall accept or reject as a group or individually within 3 months. Nominees will be submitted to the Senate until all vacant positions are filled and as needed thereafter.

A judge already in the position may be renominated for another term.

Subsection 1b) Behavior, Reports, Recusing

All federal judges, both of the Supreme Court and lower courts, including the Chief Justice, shall hold their offices during good behavior, free of scandal, bribes, acceptance of emoluments of greater than $100 in value, or conviction of felonies, racial, sexual, religious, ethnic, or national discrimination for a period of ten years. Each judge shall file an annual written report of all gifts totaling more than $100, and property financial transactions of more than $5,000 received by the judge, spouse, dependent, household member, or from any person, organization, political entity, business or equivalent in services, political advertising in any form of media, or any of those listed. Supreme Court judges shall submit the report to the appropriate judicial-oversight committee in Congress. Lower-court federal judges shall send the report to the court at the next highest level of the judicial system by April 15 of the next calendar year.

All federal judges must recuse themselves from any proceeding in which they, a relative, or business partner has any financial or political involvement.

Failure to comply, except for serious illness, shall be cause for immediate resignation, impeachment, or dismissal.

Subsection 1c) Compensation and Retirement

Judges, both of the Supreme and lower federal courts, shall, at stated times, receive for their services, a compensation, which shall not be diminished during their continuance in office. Each judge shall also receive Social Security Retirement payments for service, if enrolled and meeting all Social Security criteria upon reaching the age authorized for others to begin receiving Social Security Retirement payments. The amount of retirement compensation for a judge shall be 1.25% of base pay for each 6 months served as a federal judge up to but not exceeding 100% of the highest base payment while in active service.

Congress shall have the power to change or amend these provisions by law or amendment.

Section 2: Powers of the Judicial Branch

Subsection 2a) Judging Constitutionality of American Laws
The Supreme Court shall have jurisdiction in cases involving the Constitutionality of any State or Federal law. States, or State Courts, may not pass or enforce any law expanding, diminishing, attempting to interpret, or in violation of the Federal Constitution.

Subsection 2b) Limitations on Interpretation and Duty to Report Unconstitutionality to Congress.
The intent of federal laws initiated in and passed by both houses of Congress can be best known by the members of Congress who made the law. If the law is declared unconstitutional by any federal court, that court shall notify both houses of Congress and the President of any and all parts of a law it believes are unconstitutional, the reasons and issues, and any corrective actions that are necessary, in its opinion. Congress may intercede at this or any level, or wait for a final Supreme Court decision.

This does not empower the courts at any level to make law by declaring parts of any law or case precedent as equal to a new law; that is the sole power of Congress.

Subsection 2c) Disputed Constitutionality Cases Can Become Amendments
The Congress can dispute a decision by the Supreme Court by amending and passing the amended law, or by submitting the law by a two-thirds majority vote in both houses as a Constitutional Amendment submitted directly to the States. If the law is favored by two thirds of the legislatures of the several States within two years, it shall become a Constitutional Amendment. If not approved by the several States within two years, it shall be placed on the ballot of the next national election. If a majority of voters approve of the measure in the national election, it shall become a valid Amendment to the Constitution, since,

in a true democracy, rules are ultimately determined by the will of the People they govern.

Subsection 2d) Court Decisions Do Not Become Case-Precedent Law

Case-precedent decisions in any court case shall apply only to the case in question and may not be used as justification for other cases, which must be judged on their own merits unless new Federal or State laws are enacted to encode the case precedent as law. This Constitution does not give the power to make law to any single person, any judge, including the appeals courts or even the Supreme Court; it is a sole prerogative and duty of Congress.

Subsection 2e) Constitutionality of Treaties, Cases of Admiralty, or Maritime Jurisdiction

Where the decision may be interpreted as a new law, the Supreme Court shall have the power to review the constitutionality of Treaties and cases of Admiralty and Maritime Jurisdiction when the United States may be a Party.

Subsection 2f) Controversies Between States or States or Foreign Entities and United States Citizens

The Supreme Court or a lower federal court shall have sole jurisdiction in resolving controversies between States; between a State and one or more citizens of another State; between citizens of the same State claiming lands, other real property, or goods in a different State; or between a citizen or citizens and a foreign government, entity, citizens, or subjects.

Subsection 2g) Other Duties of the Supreme Court

In all cases of foreign ambassadors, other public ministers and consuls, and those in which a State shall be a Party, the Supreme Court shall have original jurisdiction. In all other cases, the Supreme Court shall have appellate jurisdiction, both as to law and fact, with such exceptions and under such regulations as Congress shall make.

Subsection 2h) Other Trials and Impeachments
The trials of all crimes, including cases of Impeachment, shall be by jury; such trials shall be held in the judicial district where the alleged crimes shall have been committed, but when not committed within any State, the trial shall be at such place or places as the Congress may by law direct or have directed.

Section 3: Treason

Treason against the United States shall consist in levying war or insurrection against the lawful government, or to spying or espionage for, giving aid, comfort, or propaganda assistance to an enemy of the United States during peace or war. No person shall be convicted of treason unless on the testimony of two witnesses to the overt act, confession in open court, or electronic, photographic, or video recording of the act. A person may face treason and espionage charges at the same time.

The Congress shall have the power to declare the punishment of treason if other than life imprisonment without pardon or parole, and no person shall be tried for treason except during the life of the person.

ARTICLE IV
Relations Between the States

Section 1: All States Shall Accept Judicial Decisions in Other States

Full faith and credit shall be given in each State and Territory to the public acts, records, and judicial proceedings of every other State and Territory under federal jurisdiction. Congress may, by general laws, prescribe the manner in which such acts, records, and proceedings shall be proved, and the effect thereof.

Section 2: Extradition

The citizens of each State and Territory under federal jurisdiction shall be entitled to all privileges and immunities of the citizens in the States and Territories under federal jurisdiction.

A person charged in any State with treason, felony, or other crime, who shall flee from justice, and be found in another State, shall, on demand of the Executive Authority of the State from which he fled, be delivered up, and be removed to the State having jurisdiction over the crime, for a trial to be held within one year from the date surrendered, and, if found innocent, shall be immediately released.

No person held for service, imprisonment, or labor in one State as punishment being found guilty in a court of law, shall, in consequence of any law or regulation therein be discharged from such service, imprisonment, or labor, but shall be delivered up and be removed to the State having jurisdiction over the crime.

Section 3: Formation of and Admission of New States

New States may be admitted by the Congress into this Union, but no new State shall be formed or erected within the jurisdiction of any other State, or any State be formed by the junction of two or more States or parts of States, without the consent of the legislatures of the States and three quarters of the citizens of voting age concerned, as well as the roll-call vote of three quarters of both Houses of Congress.

The Congress shall have the power to dispose of and make all needful rules and regulations respecting the Territories or other property belonging to the United States; nothing in this Constitution shall be so construed as to prejudice any claims of the United States or of any particular State.

Section 4: Federal Responsibility to the States

The United States shall guarantee to every State in this Union a Democratic Republican form of government, and shall protect each of them against invasion, and on application of the legislature, or of the Executive, when the legislature cannot be convened in sufficient time, against domestic violence.

Section 5: Withdrawal or Removal of a State from the Union

Since States have been admitted to the Union by request and consent of the territory and citizens thereof, and with the consent of the legislatures of the States concerned as well as Congress, and in order to allow the peaceful withdrawal or removal of a State and its willing citizens to sever all relations, rights, responsibilities, and benefits of membership in the United States of America, a State or territory may do so on the first day of the following calendar year if 12 or more months intervene from the date of the submission of the request to withdraw, and if all of the following conditions are met:

    a. The Executive and three quarters of both Houses of the State or Territory's legislature wishing to depart must, by roll-call vote, petition the Congress of the United States to do so;

    b. At least three quarters of citizens of federal voting age must, in a free and fair election, agree to the petition before it is submitted to Congress;

    c. All citizens wishing to depart the State before or after it secedes must be given the opportunity to freely do so, taking whatever possessions they own with them;

    d. All citizens choosing to depart must be paid fair compensation as determined by a federal court of the United States for any real property or possession they are unable to remove when they depart;

e. The State shall surrender to the United States all equipment and weapons of war within that State and pay fair compensation to the United States Treasury as determined by a federal court of the United States for all federal property and equipment that cannot be removed by the federal government, including but not limited to, known mineral rights and natural resources on federal lands, national parks, buildings and structures, roads, dams, power-generating, -storage, and -transmission structures and equipment and bridges, except for any paid for entirely with State funds.

f. Both Houses of Congress shall agree to all terms and conditions of the withdrawal by a roll-call vote of approval by three quarters of the members of both Houses, excepting and not counting the current Members of both Houses representing the State seeking removal in any of the calculations or votes.

g. Congress may remove any State that participates in insurrection or seeks to undermine any lawful and free federal election by a three-quarters vote of approval of the Members of both Houses and impose any or all of the conditions in Section 5, above.

Article V
Amending This Constitution

The Congress, whenever two thirds of both Houses shall deem it necessary, shall propose Amendments to this Constitution, or on the application of the legislatures of two thirds of the several States, shall call a Convention for proposing Amendments, which, in either case, shall be valid to all intents and purposes, as part of this Constitution, when ratified by the legislatures of three fourths of the several States, or by Conventions in three fourths thereof, as one or the other mode of ratification may be proposed by the Congress. If one percent of the registered voters sign a petition to put a Proposition for a Constitutional Amendment on the federal ballot and present it to the President of the Senate, the Proposition shall be placed on the ballot of the next federal election and if passed by a simple majority of votes, it shall become an Amendment to this Constitution and become effective at 00:01 on the first day of January of the next calendar year.

ARTICLE VI
Debts, Treaties, and Existing Laws

All debts contracted and engagements entered into, before the Adoption of this Constitution, shall be as valid against the United States under this Constitution, as under the previous Constitution.

This Constitution, and the laws of the United States which shall be made pursuant thereof; and all treaties previously made, or which shall be made, under the authority of the United States, shall be the Supreme Law of the Land; and the Supreme Court and the judges in every State shall be bound thereby, unless declared unconstitutional by the Supreme Court and not overturned by Congress or a plebiscite of the people, anything in the Constitution or laws of any State to the contrary notwithstanding.

The aforementioned Senators and Representatives, the Members of the State legislatures, and executives and judicial officers, both of the United States and of the several States, shall be bound by the Oath of Affirmation, to support this Constitution. Failure to do so may be subject to impeachment investigation by a twelve-member committee by either House of Congress or State legislature acting as a Grand Jury, with subpoena and investigative authority, and, by majority vote, referral to a Federal or State court of law, as appropriate, for a trial by jury of twelve citizens and four alternates of voting age. Conviction by unanimous vote shall result in immediate dismissal from office, possible incarceration, parole, or fines.

Article VII
Ratification of the Modern Constitution for the 21st Century

The ratification of three quarters of the existing State legislatures shall be sufficient for the establishment of this Constitution between the existing States, or if ratification has not occurred by the next national election, the measure shall be placed on the ballot as a Proposition measure to adopt this modernization to the Constitution by a simple majority of the voting citizens in a national plebiscite as deliniated in Article V.

Article VIII
Bill of Rights of all Citizens and Permanent Residents

Subsection 1a) Freedom of Religion
Neither Congress nor any State shall make any law with respect to an establishment of religion or the expression or exercise thereof, or of religious free speech except if it impinges on the freedom of others or advocates commission of a crime, violence toward others or any institution of government. There shall be no nationally endorsed religion in the United States. No religious test shall ever be required as a qualification to any office or public trust under the authority of the United States or any State.

Subsection 1b) Freedom of Speech
Neither Congress nor any State shall make any law respecting freedom of expression of political or any other views or opinions, provided that they are not false or are verifiable as true. Congress shall be empowered to make any necessary laws to prevent the dissemination of unverifiable

propaganda, rumors, exaggerations, conspiracy theories, advertisements, videos or recordings, or speeches containing known falsehoods that can damage or destroy a person's or an institution's reputation, or hinder someone's ability to pursue happiness—or even get a fair trial.

Subsection 1c) Freedom of the Press and Media

Neither Congress nor any State shall make any law restricting printed, broadcast, or recorded media with regard to freedom of expression or views, except for disseminating unlawful propagandizing of information, images, or altered communications known to be false, reports or rumors damaging to the reputation of any person or entity unless verifiable as true, and pictures or graphics violating privacy without signed permission of every person in the material unless more than six people are easily identifiable. Recording the material for possible evidence of an unlawful act is permitted.

Subsection 1d) Freedom of Assembly

Neither Congress nor any State shall make any law restricting freedom of assembly except in areas that compromise public safety or freedom of travel, and inside public facilities where documents pertaining to national security may be stored or in use, or if the assembly advocates violence against any person or public institutions.

Subsection 1e) Freedom of Petition

Neither Congress nor any State shall make any law restricting peaceful freedom of petition of grievances or outlawing any political party or movement, unless it advocates or encourages violent change in the government or any if its institutions.

Subsection 1f) Right to Bear Arms

Weapons of war deemed by Congress to be necessary for national security and safety shall be regulated and limited to military, law enforcement, National Guard, and other personnel necessary for public safety or national security. A militia of the People, well-regulated by the government of the People, being necessary to the security of a free State, the right of the people to keep and bear arms, but not weapons of war, for self-protection and sport shall not be infringed, except to prevent unlawful harm to other citizens or commission of criminal acts.

Congress shall have the authority to make such laws governing the ownership, licensing, storage, and use of arms for self-protection and sport.

Subsection 1g) Housing of Military and Law-Enforcement Personnel

No military, law-enforcement, or militia personnel shall be quartered in any house during peace or war, without the consent of the owner, and then only in a manner to be prescribed by law.

Subsection 1h) Citizen Rights to Privacy, Security, and Unreasonable Searches and Seizures

The right of the People to be secure in their persons, privacy of information, houses, papers, and effects from searches, seizures, or dissemination without written permission, shall not be violated, and no warrants be issued, but upon probable cause, supported by oath or affirmation, and, particularly, describing the place to be searched, the persons or things to be seized, or information to be released and a compelling reason to do so.

Subsection 1i) Self-Incrimination

Military personnel charged with a crime related to military service shall be tried by Court Martial, according to the Laws of the Military Code of Conduct and its laws and regulations. No military personnel or their legal partner shall be forced to testify against themselves or their domestic partner.

No person shall be held to answer for a capital, or otherwise infamous crime, unless on presentation of an indictment of a Grand Jury, regardless of present position or duties, but such an indictment shall be enforceable even against the President, Vice-President, Cabinet Members, Ambassadors, or Members of Congress, all of whom shall be subject to indictment and trial while in office.

No Statute of Limitations shall be made for the crimes of sexual abuse of a person younger than 18 years of age, or for rape, incest, or premeditated murder at any age.

No person shall be subject for the same offense to be put in jeopardy of life or limb except in cases of jury tampering, destruction of evidence, bribery, or compelling new evidence of unjust conviction.

No person shall be compelled in any criminal case to be a witness against himself, nor be deprived of life, liberty, or property without due process of law. No accused person or any witness shall be subjected to any physical, mental, or emotional abuse while in the presence or custody of law enforcement.

No person shall suffer the loss of private property taken for public or private use without just compensation approved by a court of law.

Section 2: Criminal Prosecutions

In all criminal prosecutions, the accused shall have the right to a speedy and public trial. "Speedy" shall mean within 6 months of arrest if incarcerated while awaiting trial. "Public" shall mean victims, the press, and media shall be allowed to record testimony and questioning in order to promote honesty and fairness in its representation to the public. Any person found innocent at trial shall be entitled to compensation for time imprisoned in a federal facility at a rate to be determined by Congress.

The jury trial shall be in the State and district wherein the crime was committed, and impartial in the opinion of the presiding judge(s). Change of venue shall be allowed only when compelling evidence is presented that the accused will not be able to receive a fair trial in the present location. Any and all appeals after conviction shall be presented at the same time and to the appeals court responsible for the area where the crime occurred, except a new appeal shall be permitted at any time when compelling evidence of innocence is discovered at a later time.

The accused shall be informed of the nature and cause of the accusation at the time of arrest or arraignment in Court and the right to counsel, and that anything said or done while in the presence of law enforcement or others can be used against the accused in a court of law. The accused shall have the right to be confronted by witnesses in person for and against the accused, or virtually when the accused has a history of violence or anger mismanagement.

The accused shall have the assistance of counsel for defense provided by the court if able to prove that adequate counsel is beyond the financial ability of the accused.

Section 3: Common-Law Cases

In suits at common law, where the value in the controversy shall exceed one hundred dollars, the right of trial by jury shall be preserved, and no proven or stipulated fact tried by the jury shall be otherwise re-examined in any court of the United States than according to the rules of the common law.

The enumeration in this constitution of certain rights shall not be construed to deny or disparage others retained by the people.

Section 4: Bail

Excessive bail shall not be required, nor excessive fines imposed, nor cruel and unusual punishments inflicted.

Section 5: Extent of Judicial Power

The judicial power of the United States shall not be construed to extend to any suit in law or equity, commenced or prosecuted against one of the United States by citizens of another State, or by citizens or subjects of a foreign state.

Section 6: Limits of This Constitution

The powers not delegated to the United States by this Constitution, nor prohibited by it to the States, are reserved to the States respectively, or to the people.

ARTICLE IX
Other Amendments and Changes in the Constitution of 1787

Section 1: Abolishing the Electoral College

Adoption of this Constitution shall immediately abolish the Electoral College. The election of the President and Vice-President of the United States and all federal elective offices shall be determined by who wins the greatest number of the votes cast by the citizens of the United States and its Territories during federal elections.

Section 2: Slavery Is Forbidden

Neither slavery nor involuntary servitude, except as a lawful punishment for crime of the party duly convicted, shall exist within any place subject to the jurisdiction of the United States.

Congress shall have the power to enforce this article by appropriate legislation.

Section 3: Citizenship by Birth and Citizens' Rights

All persons born legally or naturalized in the United States, including Native Americans and subject to the jurisdiction thereof, are citizens of the United States and of the State wherein they reside at the time of birth or naturalization unless neither parent is a U.S. citizen, but shall automatically become a citizen after residing in the United States or one of its Territories or Possessions for 12 continuous calendar months after birth. Proof of meeting these requirements shall be presented to a federal immigration office before documentation of citizenship is provided.

No State shall make or enforce any law which shall abridge the privileges or immunities of citizens of the United States, nor shall any State deprive any person of life, liberty, or property, without the due process of law; nor deny to any person within its jurisdiction the equal protection of the laws, nor the right to vote if that person who is a citizen who has reached the proper age and is not imprisoned for rebellion or a felony. Children born to an America citizen living outside the Territory subject to the authority of the United States of America shall be granted citizenship if that person meets the qualifications specified in United States law.

Section 4: Dual Citizenship Not Allowed; Representation in Congress

Representatives and Senators shall be apportioned among the several States according to their respective numbers, counting the whole number of persons in each state.

Undivided citizen loyalty precludes dual citizenship, so no United States Citizen shall have dual citizenship after this Constitution is adopted. All those who currently hold such dual citizenship must renounce all except their American citizenship and submit a notarized letter to the nearest federal office of immigration within six months that they have done so or forfeit their American citizenship.

Section 5: Right to Vote Begins at Age 18 Years

But when the right to vote at any federal election or for the Executive and Judicial officers of a State, or members of the legislature thereof, is denied to any of the inhabitants of such State, being eighteen years of age or older, and who are of the United States or its territories, or in any way abridged, except for participation in rebellion, insurrection, or other crime, the basis of representation therein shall be reduced in the proportion which the number of such citizens shall bear to the whole number of citizens eighteen years of age or older in such State.

Section 6: Not Serve in Any Public Office if Part of an Insurrection or Rebellion

No person shall be a Senator or Representative in Congress, or hold any office, civilian or military, under the United States, or under any State, who, having previously taken an oath, as a member of Congress, or as any officer of the United States, or as a member of any State legislature, or as an executive or judicial officer of any State, at any time and for any reason taken an oath to support and defend the Constitution of the United States shall have engaged in insurrection or rebellion against the same, or given aid or comfort to the enemies thereof.

Peaceful protest of a grievance being excepted.

Section 7: The National Debt

The validity of public debt of the United States, authorized by law, including debts incurred for payment of pensions and bounties for service in suppressing insurrection or rebellion, shall not be questioned. The national debt ceiling shall be raised whenever necessary to pay such debt and ensure the safety and security of any debt obligations incurred in a lawful manner by the United States.

Section 8: Illegal Debt

But neither the United States nor any State shall assume or pay any debt or obligation incurred in aid of insurrection or rebellion against the United States, or any claims for loss; but all such debts, obligations, and claims shall be held illegal and void.

Section 9: Enforcement

The Congress shall have the power to enforce, by appropriate legislation, the provisions of this article.

ARTICLE X
Voting Rights, Tax Loopholes, and The Electoral College Amendments

Section 1: Right to Vote

The right of citizens of the United States and its territories to vote shall not be denied or abridged by the United States or by any State or Territory on account of race, color, religion, or sexual orientation, or previous condition of servitude or imprisonment, if all terms, paroles, fines, restitutions, and punitive conditions have been completed.

The Congress shall have the power to enforce this article by appropriate legislation.

Section 2: Closing Taxation Loopholes

The Congress shall have the power to lay and collect taxes on incomes, from whatever source derived, without apportionment among the States, and without regard to any census or enumeration, including but not limited to the value of stock options at the value when purchased minus actual price paid, with the difference being taxed as received income in the tax year of the purchase, money borrowed from any asset, including but not limited to trusts, 401k, retirement-deferred income, annuity, education funds, and money borrowed on real estate not used for repairs or improvement to the property, shall be taxable as income in the year borrowed even if the interest is not tax deductible.

Section 3: Repeal of the 17th Amendment of the 1787 Constitution

Article X, Subsection 1 hereby repeals the 17th Amendment since this Constitution changes the number of Senators for each State, based on population, and abolishes the Electoral College.

Section 4: Repeal of the 18th Amendment of the 1787 Constitution

Article X, Subsection 2 hereby declares that the former 18th Amendment was repealed by the 21st Amendment, and, therefore, both are no longer needed and the use of intoxicating beverages is now a subject for the individual States to decide.

Section 5: Vote and Identity

The right of citizens of the United States and its territories to vote shall not be denied or abridged by the United States or any State or Territory on account of race, color, religion, or sexual identity.

ARTICLE XI
Amendments to the 1787 Constitution

Section 1: Beginning of Terms of Office

The terms of the President and Vice President shall end at noon on the 20th day of January, and the terms of Senators and Representatives at noon on the 3rd day of January, of the years specified in this Constitution, and the terms of their successors shall then begin.

Section 2: Start of Congressional Sessions

The Congress shall assemble at least once in every year, and such meeting shall begin at noon on the 3rd day of January, unless they shall by law appoint a different day.

Section 3: Succession in Executive Branch
if President-Elect Dies

If, at the time fixed for the beginning of the term of President, the President-Elect shall have died, the Vice-President-Elect shall become the President. If a President shall not have been chosen before the time fixed for the beginning of the term, or if the President-Elect shall have failed to qualify, then the President in office shall continue to be temporary President and shall, by Executive Order, have a new election held 30 days after the vacancy occurred and the President and

Vice-President shall temporarily continue the duties of those offices for 90 days and extended an additional 30 days until both the offices are filled in a new election. If no qualified candidate is elected to each office, a second national election shall be held in 30 calendar days, and if no qualified candidate is elected to each office, this process shall be repeated every 30 calendar days until qualified persons are elected to both offices.

Section 4: Death of the Speaker of the House or President of the Senate (Vice-President)

The Congress may, by law, provide for the case of the death of any of the persons from whom the House of Representatives may choose a Speaker whenever the right choice shall have devolved upon them, but for the case of the vacancy of President of the Senate, the majority leader of the Senate shall assume the duties and responsibilities of the Vice-President until a new Vice-President is elected. A national election shall be declared by the President, by Executive Order, for that purpose including only candidates of the same political party as the President and occur within 90 days of the vacancy of the office of the Vice-President and once every 30 days thereafter until a qualified new Vice-President is elected.

Section 5: 21st Amendment to the 1787 Constitution

The 18th Article of Amendment to the Constitution of 1787 of the United States is hereby repealed.

Section 6: Limitation of the Presidency to two terms (22nd Amendment to the 1787 Constitution)

No person shall be elected to the office of President more than twice, and no person who has held the office of president, or acted as President, for more than two years of a term to which some other person was elected President, shall be elected to the Office of President more than once. But this article shall not apply to any person holding the office of President when this Article was proposed to Congress and shall not prevent any person who may be holding the office of President, or acting as President, during the term within which this Article becomes operative from holding the office of President or acting as President during the remainder of such term.

This provision is added to this Constitution by this Section.

Section 7: Repeal of the 23rd Amendment to the 1787 Constitution

The 23rd Amendment to the 1787 Constitution is hereby repealed since the Electoral College is abolished by Article IX, Subsection 1a, of this Constitution.

Section 8: Taxes and Voting Rights (the 24th Amendment to the 1787 Constitution)

The rights of citizens of the United States to vote in any primary or other election for President or Vice President, or for Senator or Representative in Congress, shall not be denied or abridged by the United States of any State by reason of failure to pay poll tax or other taxes related to voting rights imposed by any State.

The Congress shall have the power to enforce or change this article by appropriate legislation.

Section 9: Replacement of President or Vice-President When There Is a Vacancy (25th Amendment to the 1787 Constitution)

Sections 1 and 2 of the 25th Amendment to the 1787 Constitution are hereby repealed and replaced by Article XI, Sections 3 & 4.

ARTICLE XII
(Formerly Sections 3 and 4 of the 25th Amendment to the 1787 Constitution)

Section 1:

Whenever the President transmits to the President pro tempore of the Senate and the Speaker of the House of Representatives his written declaration that he is unable to discharge the powers and duties of his office, and until he transmits to them in a written declaration to the contrary, such powers and duties shall be discharged by the Vice President as Acting President.

Section 2

If within 120 days of the initial letter of disability the President transmits to the President pro tempore of the Senate and the Speaker of the House of Representatives, the President's written declaration that no inability exists, the President shall resume the powers and duties of the office of President unless the Vice-President and a majority of the principal officers of the Executive Branch or such other body as Congress may, by law, provide, transmit within four days to the President pro tempore of the Senate and the Speaker of the House of Representatives their written declaration that the President is still unable to discharge the powers and duties of the office. Thereupon, Congress shall decide the issue, assembling in person or virtually, with adequate safety precautions, within 48 hours for that purpose in Special Session. If the Congress determines by a two-thirds vote of both Houses that the President is unable to discharge the powers and duties of the office of President, the Vice-President shall resume the powers and duties of the Presidency and begin the procedures specified in Article XI.

Article XII

No law, varying the compensation for the services of the Senators and Representatives, shall take effect, until an election of representatives shall have intervened.

★　★　★

The United States Constitution[3] of 1787 and Its 27 Amendments Still in Use 240-Plus Years Later

Preamble

We the People of the United States, in order to form a more perfect Union, establish Justice, insure domestic Tranquility, provide for the common defense, promote the general Welfare, and secure the Blessings of Liberty to ourselves and our Posterity, do ordain and establish this Constitution for the United States of America.

The Constitutional Convention
ARTICLE I

Section 1: Congress

All legislative Powers herein granted shall be vested in a Congress of the United States, which shall consist of a Senate and House of Representatives.

Section 2: The House of Representatives

The House of Representatives shall be composed of Members chosen every second Year by the People of the several States, and the Electors in each State shall have the Qualifications requisite for Electors of the most numerous Branch of the State Legislature.

No person shall be a Representative who shall not have attained the Age of twenty-five Years, and been seven Years a Citizen of the United States, and who shall not, when elected, be an inhabitant of that State in which he shall be chosen.

Representatives and direct Taxes shall be apportioned among the several States which may be included within this Union, according to their respective Numbers, which shall be determined by adding to the whole Number of free Persons, including those bound to Service for a Term of Years, and excluding Indians not taxed, three fifths of all other Persons. The actual Enumeration shall be made within three Years after the first Meeting of the Congress of the United States, and within every subsequent Term of ten Years, in such Manner as they shall by Law direct. The number of Representatives shall not exceed one for every thirty Thousand, but each State shall have at Least one Representative: and until such enumeration shall be made, The State of New Hampshire shall be entitled to chuse three, Massachusetts eight, Rhode Island, and Providence Plantation one, Connecticut five, New York six, New Jersey four, Pennsylvania eight, Delaware one, Maryland six, Virginia ten, North Carolina five, South Carolina five, and Georgia three.

When vacancies happen in the Representation from any State, the Executive Authority thereof shall issue Writs of Election to fill such Vacancies.

The House of Representatives shall chuse their Speaker and other Officers, and shall have the sole Power of Impeachment.

Section 3: The Senate

The Senate of the United States shall be composed of two Senators from each State, chosen by the Legislature thereof, for six Years; and each Senator shall have one Vote.

Immediately after they shall be assembled in Consequence of the first Election, they shall be divided as equally as may be into three Classes. The Senators of the first Class shall be vacated at the Expiration of the second Year, of the second Class at the Expiration of the fourth Year, and of the third Class at the Expiration of the sixth Year, so that one third may be chosen every second Year, and if Vacancies happen by Resignation or otherwise, during the Recess of the Legislature of any State, the Executive thereof may make temporary Appointments until the next Meeting of the Legislature, which shall then fill such Vacancies.

No Person shall be a Senator who shall not have attained to the Age of thirty Years, and been nine Years a Citizen of the United States, and who shall not, when elected, be an inhabitant of that State for which he shall be chosen.

The Vice President of the United States shall be President of the Senate, but shall have no Vote, unless they be equally divided.

The Senate shall chuse their other Officers, and also a President pro tempore, in the Absence of the Vice President, or when he shall exercise the Office of President of the United States.

The Senate shall have the sole Power to try all Impeachments. When sitting for that Purpose, they shall be on Oath or Affirmation. When the President of the United States is tried, the Chief Justice shall preside: And no Person shall be convicted without the Concurrence of two thirds of the Members present.

Judgment in Cases of Impeachment shall not extend further than removal from Office, and disqualification to hold and enjoy any Office of honor, Trust, or Profit under the United States: but the

Party convicted shall nevertheless be liable and subject to Indictment, Trial, Judgment and Punishment, according to Law.

Section 4: Elections

The Times, Places and Manner of holding Elections for Senators and Representatives shall be prescribed in each State by the Legislature thereof, but the Congress may, at any time, by Law, make or alter such Regulations, except as to Places of chusing Senators.

The Congress shall assemble at least once in every Year, and such Meeting shall be on the first Monday in December, unless they shall by Law appoint a different Day.

Section 5: Powers and Duties of Congress

Each House shall be the Judge of the Elections, Returns, and Qualifications of its own Members, and a Majority of each shall constitute a Quorum to do Business: but a smaller Number may adjourn from day to day, and may be authorized to compel the Attendance of absent members, in such Manner, and under such Penalties as each House may provide.

Each House may determine the Rules of its Proceedings, punish its Members for disorderly Behavior, and, with the Concurrence of two thirds, expel a Member.

Each House shall keep a Journal of its Proceedings, and from time to time publish the same, except such Parts as may, in their judgment, require Secrecy; and the Yeas and Nays of Members of either House on any question shall, at the Desire of one fifth of those Present, be entered in the Journal.

Neither House, during the Session of Congress, shall, without the Consent of the other, adjourn for more than three days, nor to any Place other that in which the two Houses may be sitting.

Section 6: Rights and Disabilities of Members

The Senators and Representatives shall receive a Compensation for their Services, to be ascertained by Law, and paid by the Treasury of the United States. They shall in all Cases, except Treason, Felony, and Breach of the Peace, be privileged from Arrest during their Attendance at the Session of their respective Houses, and in going to and returning from the same; and for any Speech or Debate in either House, they shall not be questioned in any other Place.

No Senator or Representative shall, during the Time for which he was elected, be appointed to any civil Office under the Authority of the United States, which shall have been created, or Emoluments whereof shall have been encreased during such time; and no Person holding any Office under the United States, shall be a Member of either House during his Continuance in Office.

Section 7: Legislative Process

All bills for raising Revenue shall originate in the House of Representatives, but the Senate may propose or concur with Amendments on the Bills.

Every Bill which shall have passed the House of Representatives and the Senate, shall, before it becomes a Law, be presented to the President of the United States: If he approve, he shall sign it, but if not he shall return it, with his Objections to that House in which it shall have originated, who shall enter the Objections at large on their Journal, and proceed to reconsider it. If after such Reconsideration two thirds of that House shall agree to pass the Bill, it shall be sent, together with the Objections, to the other House, by which it shall likewise be reconsidered, and if approved by two thirds of that House, it shall become a Law. But in all Cases, the Votes of both Houses shall be determined by Yeas and

Nays, and the Names of the Persons voting for and against the Bill shall be entered on the Journal of each House respectively. If any Bill shall not be returned by the President within ten Days (Sundays excepted) after it shall have been presented to him, the Same shall be a Law, in like Manner as if he had signed it, unless the Congress, by their Adjournment, prevent its return, in which Case it shall not be a Law.

Every Order, Resolution, or Vote to which the Concurrence of the Senate and House of Representatives may be necessary (except on a question of Adjournment) shall be presented to the President of the United States; and before the Same shall take Effect, shall be approved by him, or being disapproved by him, shall be passed by two thirds of the Senate and House of Representatives, according to the Rules and Limitations prescribed in the Case of a Bill.

Section 8: Powers of Congress

The Congress shall have the Power To lay and collect Taxes, Duties, imposts and Excises, to Pay Debts and provide for the common Defence and general Welfare of the United States, but all Duties, Imposts and Excises shall be uniform throughout the United States;

To borrow Money on the credit of the United States;

To regulate commerce with foreign nations, and among the several States, and with the Indian Tribes;

To establish a uniform Rule of Naturalization, and uniform Laws on the subject of Bankruptcies throughout the United States;

To coin Money, regulate the Value thereof, and of foreign Coin, and fix the Standard of Weights and Measures;

To provide for the Punishment of counterfeiting the Securities and current Coin of the United States;

To establish Post Offices and post Roads;

To promote the Progress of Science and useful Arts, by securing for limited Times to Authors and inventors the exclusive Right to their Writings and Discoveries;

To constitute Tribunals inferior to the supreme Court;

To define and punish Piracies and Felonies committed on the high seas, and against the Law of Nations;

To declare War, grant Letters of Marque and Reprisal, and make Rules concerning Captures on Land and Water;

To raise and support Armies, but no Appropriation of Money to that Use shall be for longer than two Years;

To provide and maintain a Navy;

To make Rules for the Government and Regulation of land and naval Forces;

To provide for calling forth the Militia to execute the Laws of the Union, suppress Insurrections, and repel invasions;

To provide for organizing, arming, and disciplining, the Militia, and for governing such Part of them as may be employed in the Service of the United States, reserving to the States respectively, the Appointment of the Officers; and the Authority of training the Militia according to the discipline prescribed by Congress;

To exercise exclusive Legislation in all Cases whatsoever, over such District (not exceeding ten Miles square) as may, by Cession of particular States, and the Acceptance of Congress, become the Seat of the Government of the United States, and to exercise like Authority over all Places purchased by the Consent of the Legislature of the State on which the Same shall be, for the Erection of Forts, Magazines, Arsenals, dockYards, and other needful Buildings; And

To make all Laws which shall be necessary and proper for carrying into Execution the foregoing Powers, and all other Powers vested by this Constitution in the Government of the United States, or in any Department or Office thereof.

Section 9: Powers Denied Congress

The Migration or Importation of such Persons as any of the States now existing shall think proper to admit, shall not be prohibited by the Congress prior to the Year one thousand eight hundred and eight, but a Tax or duty may be imposed on such importation, not exceeding ten dollars for each Person.

The Privilege of the Writ of Habeas Corpus shall not be suspended, unless when the Cases of Rebellion or Invasion the public Safety may require it.

No Bill of Attainder or *ex post facto* Law shall be passed.

No Capitation, or other direct, Tax shall be laid, unless in Proportion to the Census or Enumeration herein before directed to be taken.

No Tax or Duty shall be laid on Articles exported from any State.

No Preference shall be given by any Regulation of Commerce or Revenue to the Ports of one State over those of another, nor shall Vessels bound to, or from, one State, be obliged to enter, clear, or pay Duties in another.

No Money shall be drawn from the Treasury, but in Consequence of Appropriations made by Law; and a regular Statement and Account of the Receipts and Expenditures of all public Money shall be published from time to time.

No Title of Nobility shall be granted by the United States: And no Person holding any Office of Profit or Trust under them, shall, without the Consent of the Congress, accept any present, Emolument, Office, or Title, of any kind whatever, from any King, Prince, or foreign State.

Section 9: Powers Denied to the States

No State shall enter into any Treaty, Alliance, or Confederation; grant Letters of Marque and Reprisal, coin money, emit Bills of Credit, make any Thing but gold and silver Coin a Tender in Payment of Debts, pass any Bill of Attainder, ex post facto Law, or Law impairing the Obligation of Contracts, or grant any Title of Nobility.

No State shall, without the Consent of Congress, lay any Imposts or Duties on Imports or Exports, except what may be absolutely necessary for executing its inspection Laws, and the net Produce of all Duties and Imposts, laid by any State on imports and Exports, shall be for the Use of the Treasury of the United States; and all such Laws shall be subject to the Revision and Control of the Congress.

No State shall, without the consent of Congress, lay any Duty of Tonnage, keep Troops or Ships of War in time of Peace, enter into any Agreement or Compact with another State, or with a foreign Power, or engage in War, unless actually invaded, or in imminent Danger as will not admit for delay.

ARTICLE II

Section 1

The executive Power shall be vested in a President of the United States of America.

He shall hold his Office during the Term of four Years, and, together with the Vice-President, be chosen for the same Term, be elected, as follows:

Each State shall appoint, in such Manner as the Legislature thereof may direct, a Number of Electors, equal to the whole Number of Senators and Representatives to which the State may be entitled in Congress, but no Senator or Representative, or Person holding an Office of Trust or Profit under the United States, shall be appointed an Elector.

The Electors shall meet in their respective States and vote by Ballot for two Persons, of whom at least one shall not be the inhabitant of the same State with themselves. And they shall make a List of all the Persons voted for, and of the Number of Votes for each, which List they shall sign and certify, and transmit to the Seat of the Government of the United States, directed to the President of the Senate. The President of the Senate shall, in the Presence of the Senate and House of Representatives, open all the Certificates, and the Votes shall be counted. The Person having the greatest Number of Votes shall be the President, if such Number be a Majority of the whole Number of Electors appointed: and if there be more than one who have such a Majority, and have an equal Number of Votes, then the House of Representatives shall immediately chuse by Ballot one of them for President: and if no Person have a Majority, then from the five highest on the List, the said House shall in like Manner chuse the President. But in chusing the President, the Votes shall be taken by States, the Representation from each State having one Vote; A quorum for this Purpose shall consist of a Member or Members from two thirds of the States, and a Majority of all the States shall be necessary to a Choice. In every Case, after the Choice of the President, the Person having the greatest Number of Votes of the Electors shall be the Vice President. But if there should remain two or more who have equal Votes, the Senate shall chuse from them by Ballot the Vice-President.

The Congress may determine the Time of chusing the Electors, and the Day on which they shall give their Votes, which Day shall be the same throughout the United States.

No Person except a natural born Citizen, or a Citizen of the United States, at the time of the Adoption of this Constitution, shall be eligible to the Office of President; neither shall any person be eligible to that Office who shall not have attained the Age of thirty-five Years and been fourteen Years a Resident within the United States.

In Case of the Removal of the President from Office, or his Death, Resignation, or inability to discharge the Powers and Duties of the said Office, the Same shall devolve to the Vice-President, and the Congress may, by Law, provide for the Case of Removal, Death, Resignation, or Inability, both of the President and Vice President, declaring such Officer shall act as President, and such Officer shall act accordingly, until the Disability be removed, or a President shall be elected.

The President shall at Times, receive for his Services, a Compensation, which shall neither be increased nor diminish during the Period for which he shall have been elected, and he shall not receive within that Period any other Emolument from the United States, or any of them.

Before he enter on the Execution of his Office, he shall take the following Oath of Affirmation: "I do solemnly swear (or affirm) that I will faithfully execute the Office of President of the United States, and will to the best of my Ability, preserve, protect and defend the Constitution of the United States."

Section 2

The President shall be Commander-in-Chief of the Army and Navy of the United States, and of the Militia of the several States, when called into the actual Service of the United States; he may require the Opinion, in writing, of the principal Officer in each of the executive Departments, upon any Subject relating to the Duties of their respective Offices, and he shall have Power to grant Reprieves and Pardons for Offenses against the United States, except in Cases of Impeachment.

He shall have Power, by and with the Advice and Consent of the Senate, to make Treaties, provided two thirds of the Senators present concur: and he shall nominate and, by and with the Advice and Consent of the Senate, shall appoint Ambassadors, other public Ministers and Consuls, Judges of the supreme Court, and all other Officers of the United States, whose Appointments are not herein otherwise provided for, and which shall be established by Law: but Congress may by Law vest the Appointment of inferior Officers, as they think proper, in the President alone, in the Courts of Law, or in the Heads of Departments.

The President shall have Power to fill up all Vacancies that may happen during Recess of the Senate, by granting Commissions, which shall expire at the End of the next Session.

Section 3

He shall, from time to time give to Congress Information of the State of the Union, and recommend to their Consideration such Measures as he shall judge necessary and expedient; he may, on extraordinary Occasions, convene both Houses, or either of them, and in Case of Disagreement between them, with respect to time of Adjournment, he may adjourn them to such Time as he shall think proper; he shall receive Ambassadors and other public Ministers; he shall take Care that the Laws be faithfully executed, and shall Commission all the Officers of the United States.

Section 4

The President, Vice President and all civil Officers of the United States, shall be removed from Office on Impeachment for, and Conviction of, Treason, Bribery, or other high Crimes and Misdemeanors.

ARTICLE III

Section 1

The judicial Power of the United States shall be vested in one supreme Court and in such inferior Courts as the Congress may, from time to time ordain and establish. The Judges, both of the supreme and inferior Courts, shall hold their Offices during good Behaviour, and shall, at stated Times, receive for their Services, a Compensation, which shall not be diminished during their Continuance in Office.

Section 2

The judicial Power shall extend to all Cases, in Law and Equity, arising under this Constitution, the Laws of the United States, and Treaties made, or which shall be made, under their Authority; —to all Cases affecting Ambassadors, other public Ministers and Consuls; —to all Cases of admiralty and maritime Jurisdiction; —to Controversies to which the United States shall be a Party; —to Controversies between two or more States; —between a State and Citizens of another State; between Citizens of different States; —between Citizens of the same State claiming Lands under Grants of different States, and between a State, or the Citizens thereof, and foreign States, citizens or Subjects.

In all Cases affecting Ambassadors, other public Ministers and Consuls, and those in which a State shall be Party, the supreme Court shall have original Jurisdiction. In all the other Cases before mentioned, the supreme Court shall have appellate Jurisdiction, both as to Law and Fact, with such Exceptions, and under such Regulations as the Congress shall make.

The Trial of all Crimes, except in Cases of Impeachment shall be by Jury; and such Trial shall be held in the State where the said Crimes shall have been committed; but when not committed in any State, the Trial shall be at such Place or Places as the Congress may by Law have directed.

Section 3

Treason against the United States shall consist only in levying War against them, or in adhering to their Enemies, giving them Aid and

Comfort. No Person shall be convicted of Treason unless on the Testimony of two Witnesses to the same overt Act, or on Confession in open Court.

The Congress shall have the Power to declare the Punishment for Treason, but no Attainder of Treason shall work Corruption of Blood, or Forfeiture except during the Life of the Person attainted.

Article IV

Section 1

Full Faith and Credit shall be given in each State to the public Acts, Records, and judicial Proceedings of every other State. And the Congress may by general Laws, prescribe the Manner in which such Acts, Records and Proceedings shall be proved, and the Effect thereof.

Section 2

The Citizens of each State shall be entitled to all Privileges and Immunities of Citizens in the several States.

A Person charged in any State with Treason, felony, or other Crime, who shall flee from Justice and be found in another State, shall on Demand of the executive Authority of the State from which he fled, be delivered up, to be removed to the State having Jurisdiction of the Crime.

No Person held to service or Labour in one State, under the Laws thereof, escaping into another, shall in Consequence of any Law or Regulation therein, be discharged from such Service or Labour, but shall be delivered up on Claim of the Party to whom the Service or Labour may be due.

Section 3

New States may be admitted by the Congress into this Union; but no new State shall be formed or erected within the Jurisdiction of any other State; nor any State be formed by the Junction of two or more States, or parts of States, without the Consent of the Legislatures of the States concerned as well as of the Congress.

The Congress shall have the Power to dispose of and make all needful Rules and Regulations respecting the Territory or other Property belonging to the United States, and nothing in this Constitution shall be so construed as to Prejudice any claims of the United States, or any particular State.

Section 4

The United States shall guarantee to every State in this Union a Republican Form of Government, and shall protect each of them against Invasion; and on Application of the Legislature, or the Executive (when the Legislature cannot be convened) against domestic violence.

ARTICLE V

The Congress, whenever two thirds of both Houses shall deem it necessary, shall propose Amendments to this Constitution, or, on the Application of the Legislature of two thirds of the several States, shall call a Convention for proposing Amendments, which, in either Case, shall be valid to all Intents and Purposes, as Part of this Constitution, when ratified by the Legislatures of three fourths of the States, or by Conventions in three fourths thereof, as the one or the other Mode of Ratification may be proposed by the Congress; Provided that no Amendment which shall be made prior to the Year One thousand eight hundred and eight shall in any Manner affect the first and fourth Clauses in the Ninth Section of the First Article; and that no State, without its Consent shall be deprived of its equal Suffrage in the Senate.

Article VI

All Debts contracted and Engagements entered into, before the Adoption of this Constitution shall be as valid against the United States under this Constitution, as under the Confederation.

The Constitution and the Laws of the United States which shall be made in Pursuance thereof and all Treaties made, or shall be made, under the Authority of the United States, shall be the supreme Law of the Land; and the Judges in every State shall be bound thereby, any Thing in the Constitution or Laws of any State to the contrary notwithstanding.

The Senators and Representatives before mentioned, and the Members of the several State.

Legislatures, and all executive and judicial Officers, both of the United States and of the several States, shall be bound by Oath or Affirmation, to support this Constitution; but no religious Test shall ever be required as a Qualification to any Office or public Trust under the United States.

Article VII

The Ratification of the Conventions of the nine States, shall be sufficient for the Establishment of the Constitution between the States so ratifying the Same.

First Amendment

Congress shall make no law respecting an establishment of religion or prohibit the free exercise thereof; or abridging the freedom of speech, or of the press, or the right of the people peacefully to assemble, and to petition the Government for the redress of grievances.

Second Amendment

A well regulated Militia, being necessary to the security of a free State, the right of the people to keep and bear Arms, shall not be infringed.

Third Amendment

No Soldier shall, in time of peace be quartered in any house, without the consent of the Owner, nor in time of war, but in a manner to be prescribed by law.

Fourth Amendment

The right of the people to be secure in their persons, houses, papers, and effects, against unreasonable searches and seizures, shall not be violated, and no Warrants shall issue, but upon probable cause, supported by Oath or affirmation, and particularly describing the place to be searched and the persons to be seized.

Fifth Amendment

No person shall be held to answer for a capital, or otherwise infamous crime, unless on a presentment or indictment of a Grand Jury, except in cases arising in the land or naval forces, or in a Militia, when in actual service in time of War or public danger; nor shall any person be subject for the same offense to be twice put in jeopardy of life or limb; nor shall he be compelled in any criminal case to be a witness against himself, nor be deprived of life, liberty, or property, without the due process of law, nor shall private property be taken for public use, without just compensation.

Sixth Amendment

In all criminal prosecutions, the accused shall enjoy the right to a speedy and public trial, by an impartial jury of the State and district wherein the crime shall have been committed, which district shall have previously ascertained by law, and to be informed of the nature and cause of the accusation against him; to have compensatory process for obtaining witnesses in his favor, and to have the Assistance of Counsel for his defence.

Seventh Amendment

In suits of common law, where the value in controversy shall exceed twenty dollars, the right to trial by jury shall be preserved, and no fact tried by a jury, shall be otherwise reexamined in any Court of the United States than according to the rule of the common law.

Eighth Amendment

Excessive bail shall not be required, nor excess fines imposed, nor cruel and unusual punishments be inflicted.

Ninth Amendment

The enumeration in the Constitution, of certain rights, shall not be construed to deny or disparage others retained by the people.

10th Amendment

The powers not delegated to the United States by the Constitution nor prohibited by the States, are reserved for the States respectfully, or to the people.

11th Amendment

The Judicial power of the United States shall not be construed to extend to any suit in law or equity, commenced or prescribed against one of the United States by Citizens of another State, or by Citizens or Subjects of any Foreign State.

12th Amendment

The Electors shall meet in their respective states and vote by ballot for President and Vice President, one of whom, at least, shall not be an inhabitant of the same state with themselves; they shall name in their ballots the person voted for as President, and in district ballots the person voted for as Vice President, and they shall make distinct lists of all persons voted for as President, and all persons voted for as Vice President, and the number of votes for each, which lists they sign and certify, and transmit sealed to the seat of the government of the United States, directed to the President of the Senate; —The President of the Senate shall, in the presence of the Senate and House of Representatives, open all the certificates, and the votes shall be counted;— The person having the greatest number of votes for President shall be the President, if such number be a majority of the whole number of Electors appointed; and if no person have such a majority, then, from the persons having the highest numbers not exceeding three on the list of those voted for as President, the House of Representatives shall choose immediately, by ballot, the President. But in choosing the President, the votes shall be taken by states, the representative from each state having one vote; a quorum for this purpose shall consist of a member or members from two-thirds of the states, and a majority of all the states shall be necessary to a choice. And if the House of Representatives shall not choose a President whenever the right of choice shall devolve to them, before the fourth day of March next following, then the Vice-President shall act as President, as in the case of death or other constitutional disability of the President. — The person having the greatest number of votes as Vice-President, shall be the Vice-President, if such number be a majority of the whole number of Electors appointed, and if no person have a majority, then from the two highest numbers on the list, the Senate shall choose the Vice-President; a quorum for the purpose shall consist of two thirds of the whole number of Senators, and the majority of the whole number shall be necessary to a choice. But no person constitutionally ineligible to the office of President shall be eligible to that of Vice-President of the United States.

13th Amendment

Section 1

Neither slavery nor involuntary servitude, except as a punishment for crime whereof the party shall have been duly convicted, shall exist in the United States, or any place subject to their jurisdiction.

Section 2

Congress shall have the power to enforce this article by appropriate legislation.

14th Amendment

Section 1

All persons born or naturalized in the United States and subject to the jurisdiction thereof, are citizens of the United States and of the State wherein they reside. No State shall make or enforce any law which shall abridge the privileges or immunities of citizens of the United States, nor shall any State deprive any person of life, liberty, or property, without due process of law, nor deny to any person within its jurisdiction the equal protection of the laws.

Section 2

Representatives shall be apportioned among the several States according to their respective numbers, counting the whole number of persons in each state, excluding Indians not taxed. But when the right to vote at any election for the choice of electors for President and Vice-President of the United States, Representatives in Congress, the Executive and Judicial officers of a State, or members of the Legislature thereof, is denied to any of the male inhabitants of such State being twenty-one years of age, and citizens of the United States, or in any way abridged, except for participation in rebellion, or other crime, the basis of representation therein shall be reduced in the proportion which the number of such male citizens shall bear to the whole number of male citizens twenty-one years of age in such State.

Section 3

No person shall be a Senator or Representative in Congress, or elector of President and Vice-President, or hold any office, civil or military, under the United States, or under any State, who having previously taken an oath, as a member of Congress, or any State legislature, or as an executive or judicial officer of any State, to support the Constitution of the United States, shall have engaged in insurrection or rebellion against the same, or given aid or comfort to the enemies thereof. But Congress may by a vote of two-thirds of each House, remove such disability.

Section 4

The validity of the public debt of the United States, authorized by law, including debts incurred for payment of pensions and bounties for services in suppressing insurrection or rebellion, shall not be questioned. But neither the United States nor any State shall assume any debt or obligation incurred in aid of insurrection or rebellion against the United States, or any claim for loss or emancipation of any slave; but all such debts, obligations, and claims shall be held illegal and void.

Section 5

The Congress shall have the power to enforce, by appropriate legislation, the provisions of the article.

15th Amendment

Section 1

The right of citizens of the United States to vote shall not be denied or abridged by the United States or any State on account of race, color, or previous condition of servitude.

Section 2

The Congress shall have the power to enforce this article by appropriate legislation.

16th Amendment

The Congress shall have the power to lay and collect taxes on incomes, from whatever source derived, without apportionment among the several States, and without regard to any census or enumeration.

17th Amendment

The Senate of the United States shall be composed of two Senators from each State, elected by the people thereof, for six years; and each Senator shall have one vote. The electors in each State shall have the qualifications requisite for electors of the most numerous branch of the State legislatures.

When vacancies happen in the representation of any State in the Senate, the executive authority of such State shall issue writs of election to fill such vacancies, Provided the legislature of any State may empower the executive thereof to make temporary appointments until the people fill the vacancies by election as the legislature may direct.

This amendment shall not be so construed as to affect the election or term of any Senator chosen before it becomes valid as part of the Constitution.

18th Amendment

Section 1

After one year from the ratification of this article the manufacture, sale, or transportation of intoxicating liquors within, the importation thereof into, the exportation thereof from the United States and all territory subject to the jurisdiction thereof for beverage purposes is hereby prohibited.

Section 2

The Congress and the several States have concurrent power to enforce this article by appropriate legislation.

Section 3

This article shall be inoperative unless it shall have been ratified as an amendment to the Constitution by the legislatures of the several States, as provided in the Constitution, within seven years from the date of the submission hereof to the States by the Congress.

19th Amendment

The right of citizens of the United States to vote shall not be denied or abridged by the United States or by any State on account of sex.

The Congress shall have the power to enforce this article by appropriate legislation.

20th Amendment

Section 1

The terms of the President and Vice President shall end at noon on the 20th day of January, and the terms of Senators and Representatives at noon on the 3d day of January, of the years in which such terms would have ended if this article had not been ratified; and the terms of their successors shall then begin.

Section 2

The Congress shall assemble at least once in every year, and such meeting shall begin at noon on the 3d day of January, unless they shall by law appoint a different day.

Section 3

If, at the time fixed for the beginning of the term of President, the President elect shall have died, the Vice-President elect shall become the President. If a President shall not have been chosen before the time fixed for the beginning of the term, or if the President elect shall have failed to qualify, then the Vice-President elect shall act as President until a President shall have qualified, and Congress may by law provide for the case wherein neither a President elect nor Vice President shall have qualified, declaring who shall act as President, or the manner in which one who is to act shall be selected, and such person shall act accordingly until a President or Vice President shall have qualified.

Section 4

The Congress may by law provide for the case of the death of any of the persons from whom the House of Representatives may choose a President whenever the right choice shall have devolved upon them, and for the case of the death of any persons from whom the Senate may choose a Vice President whenever the right choice shall have devolved upon them.

Section 5

Sections 1 and 2 shall take effect on the 15th day of October following the ratification of the article.

Section 6

This article shall be inoperative unless it shall have been ratified as an amendment to the Constitution by the legislatures of three-fourths of the several States within seven years from the date of its submission.

21st Amendment

Section 1

The eighteenth article of amendment to the Constitution of the United States is hereby repealed.

Section 2

The transportation or importation into any State, Territory, or Possession of the United States for delivery or use therein of intoxicating liquors, in violation of the laws thereof, is hereby prohibited.

Section 3

This article shall be inoperative unless it shall have been ratified as an amendment to the Constitution by conventions in the several States, as provided in the Constitution, within seven years from the date of the submission hereof to the States by Congress.

22nd Amendment

Section 1

No person shall be elected to the office of President more than twice, and no person who has held the office of President, or acted as President, for more than two years of a term to which some other person was elected President shall be elected to the office of President more than once. But this Article shall not apply to any person holding the office of President when this Article was proposed to Congress, and shall not prevent any person who may be holding the office of President, or acting as President, during the term within which this

Article becomes operative, from holding the office of President or acting as President during the remainder of such term.

Section 2

This article shall be inoperative unless it shall have been ratified as an amendment to the Constitution by the legislatures of three-fourths of the several States within seven years from the date of its submission to the States by the Congress.

23rd Amendment

Section 1

The District constituting the seat of Government of the United States shall appoint in such a manner as Congress may direct:

A number of electors of President and Vice-President equal to the whole number of Senators and Representatives in Congress to which the District would be entitled if it were a State, but in no event more than the least populous State; they shall be in addition to those appointed by the States, but they shall be considered, for the purpose of the election of President and Vice President, to be electors appointed by a State, and they shall meet in the District and perform such duties as provided by the twelfth article of Amendment.

Section 2

The Congress shall have power to enforce this article by appropriate legislation.

24th Amendment

Section 1

The rights of citizens of the United States to vote in any primary or other election for President or Vice President, for electors for President or Vice President, or for Senator or Representative in Congress, shall not be denied or abridged by the United States or any State by reason of failure to pay poll tax or other tax.

Section 2

The Congress shall have the Power to enforce this article by appropriate legislation.

25th Amendment

Section 1

In case of removal of the President from office or of his death or resignation, the Vice President shall become President.

Section 2

Whenever there is a vacancy in the Office of Vice President, the President shall nominate a Vice President who shall take office upon confirmation by a majority vote of both Houses of Congress.

Section 3

Whenever the President transmits to the President pro tempore of the Senate and the Speaker of the House of Representatives his written declaration that he is unable to discharge the powers and duties of his office, and until he transmits to them in a written declaration to the contrary, such powers and duties shall be discharged by the Vice President as Acting President.

Section 4

Whenever the Vice-President and a majority of either the principal officers of the executive departments or of such other body as Congress may by law provide, transmit to the President pro tempore of the Senate and Speaker of the House of Representatives their written declaration that the President is unable to discharge the powers and duties of his office, the Vice-President shall immediately assume the powers and duties of the office as Acting President.

Thereafter, when the President transmits to the President pro tempore of the Senate and the Speaker of the House of Representatives his written declaration that no disability exists, he shall resume the powers and duties of his office unless the Vice-President and a majority of either the principal officers of the executive departments or such other body as Congress may by law, provide, transmit within four days to the President pro tempore of the Senate and the Speaker of the House of Representatives their written declaration that the President is unable to discharge the powers and duties of his office. Thereupon Congress shall decide the issue, assembling within forty-eight hours for that purpose if not in session. If the Congress, within twenty-one days after receipt of the latter written declaration, or, if Congress is not in session, within twenty-one days after the Congress is required to assemble, determines by two-thirds vote of both Houses that the President is unable to discharge the powers and duties of his office, the Vice-President shall continue to discharge the same as Acting President; otherwise, the President shall resume the powers and duties of his office.

26th Amendment

Section 1

The right of citizens of the United States, who are eighteen years of age or older, to vote shall not be denied or abridged by the United States or by any State on account of age.

Section 2

The Congress shall have the Power to enforce this article by appropriate legislation.

27th Amendment

No law, varying the compensation for the services of the Senators and Representatives shall take effect until an election of representatives shall have intervened.

★ ★ ★

Endnotes

Chapter 2

1.) The George Washington Presidential Library at Mount Vernon; *Proclamation Line of 1763. Internet article.*

2.) University of Rochester News Center: Arthur R. Miller, Professor of History, *Independence: The Tangled Roots of the American Revolution,* book author 2014 (http:// www.rochester.edu/research/research-connection/June-06-2014.htnl,

Chapter 9

3.) US. Department of Commerce U.S. Census Bureau 2020 Census

Chapter 21

4.) National Constitutional Center, 525 Arch Street, Philadelphia, PA, 19106

www.ingramcontent.com/pod-product-compliance
Lightning Source LLC
Chambersburg PA
CBHW071739150726
47998CB00005B/1711